The Limits of Hope and the Logic of Love

Essays on Eschatology and Social Action

The Limits of Hope and the Logic of Love

Essays on Eschatology and Social Action

Stephen N. Williams

with an essay response by
Miroslav Volf

REGENT COLLEGE PUBLISHING
Vancouver, British Columbia

The Limits of Hope and the Logic of Love: Essays on Eschatology and Social Action
Copyright © 2006 Stephen N. Williams

All rights reserved. No part of this publication may be reproduced, stored in a retrieval system, or transmitted, in any form or by any means, electronic, mechanical, photocopying, recording or otherwise, without the prior written permission of the author, except in the case of brief quotations embodied in critical articles and reviews.

Published 2006 by Regent College Publishing
5800 University Boulevard, Vancouver, BC V6T 2E4 Canada
Web: www.regentpublishing.com
E-mail: info@regentpublishing.com

Regent College Publishing is an imprint of the Regent Bookstore <www.regentbookstore.com>. Views expressed in works published by Regent College Publishing are those of the author and do not necessarily represent the official position of Regent College <www.regent-college.edu>.

Original publication information of the articles in this volume are as follows:

'Thirty Years of Hope: A Generation of Writing on Eschatology', in K.E. Brower and M.W. Elliott, eds., *'The Reader Must Understand': Eschatology in Bible and Theology* (Leicester: Apollos, 1997).

'The Problem with Moltmann', *European Journal of Theology* 5:2 (1996): 157–167.

'The Parition of Love and Hope: Eschatology and Social Responsibility', *Transformation* 7:3 (July/September 1990): 24–27.

Miroslav Volf, 'On Loving With Hope: Eschatology and Social Responsibility', *Transformation* 7:3 (July/September 1990): 28–31.

'Evangelicals and Eschatology: A Contentious Case', in A. N. S. Lane, ed., *The Interpretation of the Bible: Historical and Theological Studies in honour of David F. Wright* (Leicester: Apollos, 1997), 259–273.

'The Limits of Love and the Logic of Love: On the Basis of Christian Social Responsibility', *Tyndale Bulletin* 41 (1989): 261–281.

Library and Archives Canada Cataloguing in Publication Data

Williams, Stephen N. (Stephen Nantlais)
The limits of hope and the logic of love: essays on eschatology and social action / Stephen N. Williams; with an essay response by Miroslav Volf.

Includes bibliographical references.
ISBN 1-57383-375-4

1. Church and social problems. 2. Love--Religious aspects--Christianity.
3. Hope--Religious aspects--Christianity. 4. Eschatology. 5. Evangelicalism.
I. Volf, Miroslav II. Title.

HN31.W45 2006   261.8088'2804   C2006-903129-0

CONTENTS

	Introduction	vii
I.	Thirty Years of Hope	13
II.	The Problem With Moltmann	35

ESCHATOLOGY AND SOCIAL RESPONSIBILITY: A DEBATE
Stephen N. Williams and Miroslav Volf

III.	*Stephen N. Williams* The Partition of Love and Hope	53
IV.	*Miroslav Volf* On Loving With Hope	65
V.	*Stephen N. Williams* Evangelicals and Eschatology: A Contentious Case	75
VI.	The Limits of Hope and the Logic of Love	93

INTRODUCTION

It is almost forty years since the translation into English of Jürgen Moltmann's *Theology of Hope*. Not only did it bring Moltmann himself to international attention; it proved to be one of the most influential theological works in the latter part of the twentieth century, as far as such things can be judged and such generalizations permitted. It sought to recapture the eschatological dimension of Christianity, interpret it aright and use it to ground a theology of social action.

It is over thirty years since the Lausanne Congress on World Evangelization. It put the mandate for social action onto the international evangelical agenda with unprecedented publicity and inaugurated what is still, one way or another, ongoing discussion on the relationship of evangelism to social action. In a consultation at Grand Rapids in 1982 which followed up Lausanne, much was debated, but the relationship of eschatology and social action proved to be a particularly divisive issue.

The essays drawn together here were first published in the nineteen-eighties and nineteen-nineties and are united by their preoccupation with the questions arising from the work of Moltmann and the intra-evangelical discussion to which I have alluded. At the time of going to press, I am very glad that the revised doctoral thesis of a former student—Tim Chester—is also going to press; Tim brings Moltmann and evangelicalism into some kind of dialogue, a task that Peter Kuzmic had thought necessary back in the days of Grand Rapids.[1]

---

[1] P. Kuzmic, 'History and Eschatology: Evangelical Views' in Bruce J. Nicholls, ed., *In Word and Deed: Evangelism and Social Responsibility* (Exeter: Paternoster,

Tim generously makes reference to most of the essays published in the present volume, but it has seemed a good idea to bring them together in a single collection, as I do here, with only minor verbal revisions of the original. The scene has changed over the last decade or two, but the issues remain with us in a form that is continuous with that of the eighties and nineties, at least in many circles.

With the exception of the first essay, the essays in this volume centre on a single thesis. I have deliberately allowed repetition to remain; careful readers will note that the formulations sometimes vary, though I hope that they are invariably consistent. I am persuaded that, if anyone is inclined to think that the thesis is repeated *ad nauseam*, at least there are worse things to get nauseous about. On the negative side, my sustained worry has been about the way in which Moltmann and many evangelicals, in their different ways, have conceived of the relationship of eschatology to social action and used the former to ground the latter. On the positive side, I attempt to sustain, in an appropriate but not an absolute way, a distinction between love and hope, grounding social action in the former rather than the latter. Hence the title of the collection. It was my original intention to write a detailed full-length treatment on this subject and a stack of folders on my shelves—over twenty, I think—stuffed with lined and handwritten sheets of paper testifies to that 'vaulting ambition' which, Shakespeare tells me, 'o'erleaped itself' (*Macbeth*. In the old days, 'folder' meant something in which you put paper and we used to write things out holding pen in hand.). Whether something will ever come of this project, I don't know; its completion would undoubtedly have made for a more satisfying product, but I hope that this short collection of essays is better than nothing.

The first essay can be ignored by those who want to go straight into the theological discussion. It is something of a literature survey, very selective of course, and rather laboured, analysed from a certain taxonomical standpoint and covering the theme of eschatology in the thirty years following the publication of the English translation of Moltmann's *Theology of Hope*. It is descriptive and does not offer a theological argument on its author's behalf. It was originally published

---

1985), 155, and Tim Chester, *Mission and the Coming of God: Eschatology, the Trinity and Mission in the Theology of Jürgen Moltmann and Contemporary Evangelicalism* (Carlisle: Paternoster, 2006).

in K. E. Brower and M. W. Elliott (eds.), *'The Reader Must Understand': Eschatology in Bible and Theology* (Leicester: Apollos, 1997).

In the second essay, I tackle the 'Problem with Moltmann', as I see it, in relation to the issue in question. As far as I am concerned, the persistent underlying problem in Moltmann's work is the consistent failure to clarify how he is using theological language. This has always struck me as leading him into much greater trouble than a friendly critic like Richard Bauckham—whose work I much admire and with whom I have had several discussions and exchanges on Moltmann in the past—will allow. It was originally published in *European Journal of Theology* (5.2) 1996.

The third essay, on the partition of love and hope, deals a little with Moltmann but moves on to the symposiasts at the Grand Rapids consultation and effects the transition to discussion of evangelical perspectives.[2] It was published in *Transformation* 7.3 (1990) and the editors requested a response from Miroslav Volf which was co-published in the same issue. I am grateful to Miroslav for permission to reprint his rejoinder which appears here in its original form as the fourth essay in this collection.

I was privileged to be one of those invited to honour Professor David Wright on the occasion of his sixty-fifth birthday and returned to the theme of 'Evangelicals and Eschatology: A Contentious Case' in a contribution to the *Festschrift* presented to him under the editorship of A. N. S. Lane, *Interpreting the Bible: Historical and Theological Studies* (Leicester: Apollos, 1997). In the course of this essay, I returned to the debate with Miroslav Volf and responded to his response. I confess that I remained unrepentant.

Finally, an earlier article is republished from *Tyndale Bulletin* 40 (1989). This was the published version of the Tyndale Lecture in Biblical Theology in 1988 and attempted to secure the grounds for social action in the context of some current counter-proposals. So the first essay reprinted here in this collection is descriptive; the central ones are polemical; this final one fittingly concludes with a more detailed constructive statement of my thesis, on biblical grounds, though the controversial note is still struck in it.

---

[2] I first engaged with the Grand Rapids report and adumbrated my thesis in an article unpublished here: 'Hope, Love and Social Action' in *Evangel* 4.3 (1986).

Twenty years—fifteen years—ten years—on, do I stand by what I have written? It is a question whose answer will probably me of interest only to me. Nevertheless, having asked it anyway, let me answer with a decisive: 'I think so'. More detailed distinctions; more phenomenological elaboration; much more in the way of constructive proposal is called for.[3] But I have found no reason to abandon the broad theological structure and, if there are burgeoning reservations, it is not yet clear to me how much effect they would have on the general thesis, if they came to full bloom.

And yet. There is a passage in the work of Abraham Kuyper that reads as follows:

> God will take delight in . . . high human development. He himself will bring it about and into view. Then he will seek in it his own glorification. The control and harnessing of nature by civilization, enlightenment, and progress, by science and art, by a variety of enterprises and industry will be entirely separate from the totally other development in holiness and integrity . . . Still, that exterior development has to continue and be completed to bring the *work of God* in our race to full visible realization. Whether or not this will subsequently be consumed in the coming cosmic conflagration does not matter. Its very completion will have sparkled before God's eye . . . And after the cosmic conflagration, that same God will once again reveal the reflection of his image in the kingdom of his glory, but then in a totally different way, that is, in complete harmony with our interior development.[4]

The harmony of cosmic conflagration with what Kuyper calls 'exterior development' is something for which I argue in what follows, albeit that I regard conflagration just as a *possibility*, if I can leave the word 'conflagration' undefined for a moment. And yet, if you will permit me one more autobiographical reference, when I first read that particular sentence ('Whether or not this will subsequently be consumed in the coming cosmic conflagration does not matter') there was a twinge of

---

[3] It is all there in the 20 folder volumes—a fact which is of interest not only to me but also to my office cleaner.

[4] I have deliberately omitted some words from this quotation, in order to avoid distraction, but the reader may care to look up the full passage. It is found in 'Common Grace' in James D. Bratt, ed., *Abraham Kuyper: A Centennial Reader* (Grand Rapids: Eerdmans; Carlisle: Paternoster, 1998), 178f.

uneasiness. I stand by my thesis but I confess that the twinge has not gone away.

I wish to acknowledge the financial support of Tyndale House and the Tyndale Fellowship in allowing me to spend a sabbatical term in Cambridge many years ago working on these themes and the trouble taken by Bill Reimer, Rob Clements and Robert Hand of Regent College Publishing, Vancouver, in producing these essays in their present form.

Stephen N. Williams
Union Theological College
Belfast

May, 2006

I

THIRTY YEARS OF HOPE
A Generation of Writing on Eschatology

This essay charts some tendencies in eschatological thought since Moltmann's Theology of Hope. *The account is thematic, rather than chronological. Moltmann's work initiated or contributed to fresh thinking about (a) the centrality, (b) the content, (c) the point and (d) the method of Christian eschatology. Correspondingly, the essay describes selected developments in these four areas. It is mostly confined to selected work in academic theology. In order to offer a fair exposition, the author does not, in this essay, enter into critical engagement with the figures and trends discussed.*

INTRODUCTION

At no point is contemporary theology more lacking in clarity and candor than in its pronouncements about the 'last things'. So writes Charley Hardwick in his recent and acclaimed *Events of Grace*.[1] He echoes a sentiment expressed just over thirty years ago by Schubert Ogden, who offered two reasons for the incredibility of standard treatments of eschatology. Firstly, eschatological statements have no sound basis in human experience or knowledge. Secondly, the mythological elements they contain lack clear conceptual meaning.

---

[1] C. Hardwick, *Events of Grace: Naturalism, Existentialism and Theology* (Cambridge: Cambridge University Press, 1996), 267f.

Ogden wrote just before the boom in theological concern with eschatology. Thirty years of hope have clearly not impressed Charley Hardwick. Without assenting to or dissenting from these judgments, two general observations are in order.

First, there seems to be less theological interest in eschatology around—at least in those academic circles that Ogden and Hardwick have in mind—than there was thirty years ago. Dermot Lane, in one of the most recent full-scale treatments of eschatology, says that 'it must be stated—and this is one of the theses of the book—that eschatology is the missing link in much contemporary theology'.[2] Thirty years ago, Moltmann and Pannenberg bore much of the responsibility for generating renewed interest in eschatology, though the interest was certainly around prior to and apart from their contribution. Possibly the publication of the last volume in Moltmann's dogmatics, which is on eschatology, and the translation of the third and final volume of Pannenberg's systematics, which also deals with eschatology, will do the trick again.[3] It remains to be seen.

Secondly, Maureen Junker-Kenny makes effective use of recent German studies of the transformation which Western societies are undergoing in the process of modernization. She highlights two characteristics relevant for the theme of hope, namely (a) people's orientation today towards the present instead of the future and (b) the loss of a common vision. 'The second feature', she notes, 'can also take the shape of an explicit farewell to utopian thinking'.[4] Doubtless one could quibble a bit on both counts, asking whether, in fact, a high proportion of people have ever been future rather than present oriented in a way that is changing now, and to what extent vision has been profoundly common in the past. But she raised important questions. Moving on from the proposition that 'it was easy to identify with the great political ideas of liberty and justice as long as one's personal hopes and the hopes

---

[2] Dermot Lane, *Keeping Hope Alive: Stirrings in Christian Theology* (Dublin: Gill & Macmillan, 1996), 5.

[3] J. Moltmann, *The Coming of God: Christian Eschatology* (London: SCM, 1996). Stanley Grenz has anticipated the translation of Pannenberg's work in *Reason for Hope: the Systematic Theology of Wolfhart Pannenberg* (New York/London: Oxford University Press, 1990).

[4] M. Junker-Kenny, ed., *Christian Resources of Hope* (Blackrock: Columbia, 1995), 29.

of humanity were still identical', she averred that 'these two levels do not coincide any more. A new ecological analysis of worldwide justice would call for self-denial. It would have to be a utopia of pure duty—for which it is hard to find enthusiastic supporters. The utopias of promise have come to an end' (p. 31f.). This impels her to ask whether hope is an enduring element of human nature or an historical legacy emanating, in the West, from Judaeo-Christianity. At any rate, it is important to restate the Christian hope in a changed context.

With this in mind, we shall survey some developments in theological eschatology in the thirty-year period from 1967 to 1997. 1967 was the publication date of the English translation of Moltmann's *Theology of Hope*, but there is more to the choice of this date than Anglophone provincialism. Even as it is, we shall but skim the surface of a selection of works. A starting point in 1964, the original date of publication of *Theology of Hope*, would let in Harvey Cox's *The Secular City*, the fifth edition of Hendrikus Berkhof's *Christ, the Meaning of History*, probably Oscar Cullmann's *Salvation in History* (though I am generally avoiding reference to biblical studies), Vatican II's *Gaudium et Spes*, not to mention the early work of Pannenberg and Rahner. However, books written before but translated after 1967, including work by Gollwitzer, Gogarten and Van Ruler, are generally ignored in what follows. Indeed, the limits are inevitably severe; I am not, for example, glancing at the discussions of eschatology that have featured in the evangelical and other systematic theologies that have flooded the market over these last three decades, nor am I touching on the themes of so-called 'individual eschatology'—life after death, the intermediate state, etc.

The title of this essay, and the preliminary remarks on its scope, involve running together two words: 'hope' and 'eschatology'. But is talk of hope necessarily eschatological talk? One characteristic of the discussions of hope and of eschatology is the attempt to relate the mundane language of hope to the language of specifically eschatological hope, so that, even if not all hope is directed to the eschaton, it is nonetheless stimulated by eschatological hope. One can also ask: is eschatology strictly about hope? For, we could speak of realized eschatology. The answer to this question is something on which Moltmann and most others in our generation have wanted to be clear; eschatology is indeed about the future, and hence its content is the potential or actual object of hope. Moltmann himself looms quite large in the following discussion. In his Ingersoll

Lecture of 1984, Pannenberg commented that the eschatological boom of the last two decades 'emerged mainly from the impact of Jürgen Moltmann's *Theology of Hope*'.[5] That sounds familiar enough, but that it should come from Pannenberg effectively banishes any reservation about giving Moltmann pride of place here.

In this volume, Moltmann attempted four things. Firstly, he affirmed the centrality of eschatology—'Christianity is eschatology'. Secondly, he affirmed its point: it is to stimulate this-worldly action. Thirdly, he affirmed its general content: it embodies promises for this world. Fourthly, he adumbrated its method: it is an exposition of christology, specifically the dialectic of cross and resurrection. We structure the survey that follows by taking these themes in turn.[6]

THE CENTRALITY OF ESCHATOLOGY

Formally, the affirmation that Christianity is eschatology did not constitute a complete novelty, although Moltmann gave it a different material content than did Barth, when Barth, in his commentary on Romans said that 'if Christianity be not altogether thoroughgoing eschatology, there remains in it no relationship whatever with Christ'.[7] Moltmann's claim was echoed by Metz, with whom Moltmann has long been associated. 'The orientation of the modern era to the future, and the understanding of the world as history, which results from this orientation, is based upon the biblical belief in the promises of God. The biblical faith demands that theology be eschatological'.[8] If Christianity is eschatological, so, naturally, is theology and in 1970 Herzog edited a whole collection entitled *The Future as Hope: Theology as Eschatology*.[9]

However they have changed, modified or supplemented their scheme over the years, the eschatological orientation of theology and

---

[5] 'Constructive and Critical Functions of Christian Eschatology', *Harvard Theological Review* 77.2 (1984): 119.

[6] For a different kind of survey covering a slightly longer period of time, see Klaas Runia, 'Eschatology in the second half of the twentieth century', *Calvin Theological Journal* 32.1 (1997): 105–135.

[7] Karl Barth, *The Epistle to the Romans* (Oxford: Oxford University Press, 1968), 314.

[8] *Theology of the World* (London: Burns & Oates, 1969), 87.

[9] (New York: Herder & Herder, 1970).

general conviction of eschatological centrality has been maintained in the work of both Moltmann and Pannenberg. An eschatological approach to theology has been influential in diverse quarters. So we find Thomas Finger, in the first volume of his *Christian Theology: An Eschatological Perspective*, appealing first and foremost to *Theology of Hope* and explicitly endorsing Moltmann's claim that 'Christianity is eschatology'.[10] In a different tradition again, Peter Jensen, Principal of Moore College in Sydney, published lectures in 1991 under the title *At the Heart of the Universe*.[11] Jensen did not speak of Moltmann's influence, but rather unexpectedly began his general exposition of Christian doctrine with eschatology. According to Jensen: 'The advantage of this procedure is that it captures the biblical sense of purpose in God and the corresponding dynamic of history'. But the concluding reason he gave in defending this procedure was that 'it makes it more likely that ethical and existential considerations will emerge from the treatment of doctrine rather than philosophical ones'.[12] That leads us on to the second characteristic of Moltmann's approach: the point of eschatology.

THE POINT OF ESCHATOLOGY

Inasmuch as theologians have emphasized the eschatological dimension of Christian faith these last thirty years or so, it has often been with a view to showing how it makes an impact on our world, specifically by stimulating, generating or steering social action and responsibility over its widest range. As Nicholas Lash put it, eschatology is a stimulant and not a narcotic.[13] He is parrying the Marxist attack on religion as an opiate and, of course, the challenge and critique of Marxism often formed the context for at least the earlier reflections on eschatology in our period.

Such was the perceived point of eschatology in the decade and more following Moltmann's *Theology of Hope*, that Ratzinger, in his 1977 publication on *Eschatology: Death and Eternal Life*, sounded a stern

---

[10] (Scottdale, PA: Herald, 1985), 101ff.

[11] (Leicester: InterVarsity Press, 1994).

[12] Ibid., 11.

[13] N. Lash, *A Matter of Hope: A Theologian's Reflections on the thought of Karl Marx* (London: Darton, Longman & Todd, 1981), 161.

warning.[14] He noted that it was possible in his day to write theological eschatology in dialogue with the theology of futurity, the theology of hope and theology of liberation. No doubt, said Ratzinger, the relation of the future to the present and the question of the praxis of hope, are parts of eschatology. But he did not intend to 'surrender to the transformation of perspectives implied in the reduction of eschatology to these things'.[15] Eschatology must continue—and major on—its reflections on death, hell, the intermediate state and immortality. Ratzinger's worry was that eschatological belief was being hijacked in a political cause. But:

> The Kingdom of God, not being itself a political concept, cannot serve as a political criterion by which to construct in a direct fashion a programme of political action and to criticize the political efforts of other people. The realisation of God's Kingdom is not itself a political process.[16]

We may insert two observations here. First, Ratzinger's reasoning is not stringent. From, 'the Kingdom of God is not a political concept' it may well follow that 'it cannot serve as a political criterion by which to construct in a direct fashion a programme of political action . . .', if we emphasize *'direct'*. But one could maintain that the kingdom is a political concept and criterion without claiming that the realization of that kingdom is a political *process.* That is, the putatively political nature of the kingdom and of criteria do not dictate a judgment on how it will be realized.

Secondly, one wishes that Ratzinger had documented his claim specifically. The kingdom of God has long been a (probably the) central eschatological concept in the work of Pannenberg and certainly in some of the material published in *Ethics* he deduces conclusions about European union from his beliefs about the eschatological unity of humankind.[17] But it is not clear that the kingdom was precisely functioning as a political concept when Pannenberg did so. And in his important essay—admittedly after the German, but prior to the English, version of Ratzinger's book—Pannenberg warned against identifying 'a

---

[14] J. Ratzinger, *Eschatology: Death and Eternal Life* (Washington, D.C.: Catholic University of America Press, 1988).

[15] Ibid., 4.

[16] Ibid., 58.

[17] (Philadelphia, PA: Westminster, 1981), chap. 7.

certain line of political action unequivocally as [even] approximating the Kingdom of God'.[18]

As for Moltmann, even when he came to his detailed exposition of 'Historical Eschatology' under the rubric of 'The Kingdom of God' in *The Coming of God*, he still did not view it as 'the integral hope of Christians'; what constitutes that is the new creation of all things.[19] Whether it was Gustafson, writing on theology and ethics, or liberation theologians, chiding European theologians of hope, the accusation was made against Moltmann that insufficiently detailed moral or political deductions were drawn from his eschatological premises and promises.[20] As for Metz, Schillebeeckx could take for granted, in this early period, that he was refusing to derive from the gospel (including its eschatological) message any direct programme of social and political action'.[21] If Ratzinger principally had liberation theologians in mind, there would have been a need to show that political conclusions were being significantly derived from eschatology, specifically kingdom eschatology.

I am not saying that Ratzinger was altogether wrong, just that examples were needed and that work was needed to show that he was right. However, it has been widely held in general, from within a whole variety of conceptual schemes in the last thirty years, that a cardinal point of eschatology is the generation of this-worldly activity. But this, of course, was a principle apparently or frequently parasitic on a particular construction of the content of eschatology, to which we now move.

THE CONTENT OF ESCHATOLOGY

The this-worldly point of eschatology derives from its this-worldly content, and with the phrase 'this-worldly' we are into real thickets of semantic ambiguity. The problems here that have arisen over the last thirty years have done so quite generally on two scores. One is the question of whether religious language in general and eschatological language in particular are being used literally, symbolically, in some combination or in some other way. The other is whether 'this-

---

[18] See the Ingersoll Lecture: 'Constructive and Critical Functions', 125.

[19] Moltmann, *The Coming of God*, 132.

[20] See below on liberation theology. For Gustafson, see *Theology and Ethics* (Oxford: Blackwell, 1981), 53–58.

[21] See Schillebeeckx, *God the Future of Man* (London: Sheed & Ward, 1969), 157.

worldly hope' refers to an ultimately eschatological state, the ultimate quasiterritorial fulfilment of hope, or to proximate hope, or to both; and, if the latter, how does or should one distinguish the usages in the literature? Further, if we are referring to ultimate hope, does it refer to a continuity between what presently is and what ultimately will be or is it compatible with a strong assertion of discontinuity (while maintaining corporeality) on a literalistic analysis? I mention this last point in our context of starting with Moltmann's concerns, because Delwin Brown, for example, in *To Set at Liberty*, quite rightly pressed the question of the meaning of 'this world' in Moltmann's theology, averring that its radical discontinuity made talk of the future of *this* world validly talk of this world only in 'a very odd sense, if at all'.[22]

Now it may be judged that either by the time Brown wrote or with *The Coming of God*, Moltmann was able to rebut the charge, but there is undoubtedly a lack of appropriate conceptual analysis in the theological eschatologies of the last thirty years. The concept of 'possibility' illustrates this. 'Hope', said Kierkegaard, 'is passion for the possible'. 'The possible' here appears terminologically to stand in contrast to 'the promised' to which specifically Christian hope, in its primary theological sense, is correlated. But it is not as simple as that. 'Possibility' can be contrasted to 'necessity'.[23] It is also semantically possible to make 'possibility' the opposite of 'impossibility' or the opposite of 'certainty'. Add the option of a technical Blochian use of the word 'possibility' and, whether one is thinking in English or in German, there is plenty of potential for confusion.

Why are the concepts surrounding hope, the concept of hope itself and of this-worldly hope, given far less analysis than they need? There are two reasons, I think.[24] First, there is a fear of dualism, a separation

---

[22] Delwin Brown, *To Set at Liberty: Christian Faith and Freedom* (Maryknoll, NY: Orbis, 1981), 116.

[23] Perhaps Ricoeur implies this in his reference to Kierkegaard: see Paul Ricoeur, 'Freedom in the Light of Hope', in *The Conflict of Interpretations: Essays on Hermeneutics* (Evanston, Ill: Northwestern University Press, 1974), 407ff.

[24] A third point would be unduly provocative. Those who work mainly within the analytic tradition of philosophical theology will note that these debates often have their provenance in theological circles little affected by that tradition and will conclude that this accounts for the general lack of stricter conceptual analysis. If this point is justified, it neither amounts to an endorsement of that tradition *tout court* nor suggests that only within it can an appropriate rigorous analysis occur.

of hopes which, by stating the distinction, will subordinate worldly concerns to avowedly ultimate ones. This has been a standard fear in the last thirty years of hope. It is reflected, for example, in the work of Dermot Lane at the end of our thirty year period. He quotes Gerald O'Hanlon: '... Our primary hope is directed towards God ... this will be realized definitively in heaven;. in a secondary sense we may hope for this-worldly anticipations of this primary hope'.[25] Lane's response would be unaffected if we were to substitute 'consummation in a new heaven and new earth' for 'heaven'. Lane said: 'To talk about primary and secondary hope runs the risk of playing down the seriousness of hope for this life'.[26] His following comments reveal the conceptual confusion involved here. What he terms 'hope for this life' may not be realized and is not, on a theological account, the object of promise. The 'hope of heaven' is a different matter, being, on a traditional theological account, a matter of certainty. The perfectly legitimate concern—that the nonproximate object of Christian hope does not rob present life and its hopes of their importance—is ill-served by blurring this distinction of hopes, however firmly we relate them. But, in Lane's analysis, there is a hint of another factor that may be responsible for the blurring of the distinction, one that also comes to light with my reference to a 'traditional account'. That is the epistemic status of things ultimately hoped for, which takes us on to the second reason.

In speaking the language of promise and certainty, one is sounding as though no epistemological questions arise in contemporary theology in relation to the knowledge of God. But, of course, they do, and questions about the grounds for hope enter into theological attempts to relate and distinguish different kinds of hope. However, much of the time they do not *systematically* enter into those attempts. Consequently, the distinction between what we may be assured will ultimately come about and what we desire will proximately come about, frequently lapses or leads a fuzzy existence. The kinds of epistemological considerations involved are indicated in Nicholas Lash's work, to which we have referred, *A Matter of Hope*.

Lash takes on Karl Popper, who attacked historicism on the grounds that 'by substituting certainty for hope, it denies man's moral

---

[25] Lane, *Keeping Hope Alive*, 123.
[26] Ibid., 128.

responsibility for the construction of his future'.[27] Lash responds that hope can be certain, but we need to explore different modes of certainty. 'In so far as hope is to be considered as a mode of knowledge of "the meaning of history", it is hermeneutic, interpretative knowledge, and not "explanation"'.[28] Later, Lash speaks of 'the knowledge to which Christian faith lays claim (which forms the substance of hope)'.[29] But Lash also contrasts hope with assertion,[30] and says that 'hope may, indeed, be questionable, but, if it is to remain hope, it can only take the form of a question. For the Christian, that question is cast as request: "Thy Kingdom come"'.[31] It is characteristic of hope never to relinquish the 'interrogative mood'.

All this risks distortion by abstraction, and it would he unfair to remark here on the coherence of Lash's exposition. I cite it as illustrative of epistemological awareness, an awareness present in Lash more than most over these last years. As for the broad content of eschatological hope, we can pick up three areas for discussion.

The Nature of This-worldliness

I have referred to and simply bracketed the question of literal and symbolic language. But talk of ultimate this-worldly hope *prima facie* involves belief in a continuity between the present and the new earth, a literal continuity which yet allows for radical transformation and symbolic representation. This whole question has been taken up with some verve in conservative evangelical discussion. In 1982, leading participants in the Lausanne movement debated the relation of evangelism to social action. The report highlighted one area of disagreement and that pertained to eschatology. Amidst general agreement on eschatological questions, there was disagreement on whether or not the new earth would be markedly continuous with this one, or whether the annihilation of this earth is in prospect. Continuity

---

[27] Lash, *A Matter of Hope*, 68.

[28] Ibid., 69.

[29] Ibid., 150.

[30] Ibid., 261.

[31] Ibid., 270.

allegedly furnished an incentive for action; the works of our hands will endure, albeit in a transformed mode.[32]

The discussion, however, is not limited to conservative evangelical circles. Moltmann, working with different methodological presuppositions, touched on it in *God in Creation* as well as in *The Coming of God*.[33] For, after all, we are dealing with a question with historical anchorage in differences between the Lutheran and the Reformed communions in the seventeenth century. Reformed theologians over the last thirty years have sustained an interest in these questions. The Dutch Calvinist tradition, in particular, has made a very prominent contribution in this area. None is more important than that of Hendrikus Berkhof. We have excluded discussion of *Christ, the Meaning of History*, whose editions were produced prior to 1967. *Well-Founded Hope*, which has escaped my ban by being published in 1969, contained some notable material, but is too scanty on the present topic to help us out.[34] But in *The Christian Faith*, translated in 1979, Berkhof, modifying a rather stronger continuist line in *Christ, the Meaning of History* wrote as follows: 'We can say that our culture provides the scaffolding for the coming structure, a scaffolding that will later be torn down again. It is also possible, however, to view our culture as providing the building materials for a coming kingdom'. He settled finally for 'the fact that all of cultural development will prove to be meaningful in the light of eternity. But that is the limit of what can be said about it'.[35]

The All-embracing Nature of Hope

Interestingly, an example of the second area to which I refer also contains a strong assertion of continuity. There has been interest in

---

[32] Grand Rapids Report, *Evangelism and Social Responsibility: An Evangelical Commitment* (Exeter: Paternoster, 1982), 40–42.

[33] *God in Creation* (London: SCM, 1985), 90–93; *The Coming of God*, 267ff.

[34] H. Berkhof, *Well-Founded Hope* (Richmond: John Knox, 1969).

[35] Berkhof, *The Christian Faith: An Introduction to the Study of the Faith* (Grand Rapids, MI: Eerdmans, 1979), 539. I correct an account in my 'Evangelicals and Eschatology: a contentious case', in A. N. S. Lane, ed., *Interpreting the Bible: Historical and Theological Studies in Honour of David Wright* (Leicester: InterVarsity Press, 1997), 291–308, where I say that Berkhof tacitly qualifies the position that he took in *Christ, the Meaning of History* (306); as a matter of fact, the qualification, if not loud, is explicit rather than tacit (518).

the all-embracing nature of this worldly hope, extending its scope to the cosmos, and going beyond hope for history to a hope for nature, matching socio-political concerns generated by hope for history with ecological concerns, generated by hope for nature.[36] The specific link with the continuity question is forged by Peter Phan in an article recently published in the *Irish Theological Quarterly*, 'Eschatology and Ecology: The Environment in the End-Time'.[37]

Phan argued that, while attention has been given to the eschatological destiny of the non-human cosmos, the 'biblical *metaphor*' of 'a new heaven and new earth' has been picked up,

> but the precise nature of the new cosmos and its relationship to the present earth are left rather vague. Indeed, it may be asked why, morally speaking, efforts, sometimes extraordinary, should be undertaken to save the environment, if in the end it will disappear, or to use a biblical metaphor, will be reduced to ashes in a universal conflagration.

Accordingly, Phan, taking up that strand in the tradition which emphasizes the intrinsic, not just the instrumental, value of the cosmos, argues for its final transformation and for its 'material and spatial' nature.

> Not only our work, especially our work of love, will remain, but also 'all creation', hence material beings included, is set to be freed from bondage to decay; it will not be destroyed nor will it disappear. 'All creation' certainly comprises more than humans; minerals, plants, animals, mountains and rivers, the heavenly bodies, the sun, the moon and the stars, from the microcosm to the macrocosm, are included in this process of liberation. In terms of St Francis' 'Canticle of the Sun', should we not think that in this 'new heavens and a new earth' there will be the same brother sun, the same sister moon, the same water and the same air? And will there not he the birds and fishes that the Poverello preached to, the bees the Saint fed with the finest sugar, the wolf he tamed, and the worms upon which he poured out the tenderest love, all of them freed from decay and sharing in eternal beatitude?

---

[36] Francis Bridger offered an evangelical contribution here in 'Ecology and Eschatology: A Neglected Dimension', *Tyndale Bulletin* 41.2 (1990): 290–301, but it was very general.

[37] 62.1 (1996): 3–16.

Human achievement will also endure. Why should the architecture of Taj Mahal or Saint Peter's Basilica, the music of Beethoven and Mozart, the tragedies of Sophocles and Shakespeare, the sculptures of Michelangelo and Rodin, the philosophies of Confucius and Plato, and the scientific discoveries of Galileo and Einstein, just to cite a few things at random, not perdure for ever?[38]

Phan's work illustrates, then, the fusion between concern for continuity and the concern regarding the implications of eschatological belief for the environment.

The God of Hope

A shift towards a cosmocentric eschatology is naturally, though not necessarily, associated with a revisionary doctrine of God. In a work like Ruether's *Gaia and God: An Ecofeminist Theology of Earth Healing*, anything like a traditional eschatology has effectively disappeared, but she was explicit on the restructuring of theology many years before that.[39] Whether or not it is particularly connected with cosmocentrism, the content of this-worldly hope in the last thirty years is frequently linked with some revisionary notions of deity.

Moltmann, in *Theology of Hope*, picked up Bloch's phrase about God as one with 'future as his essence', although I think that the significance for *Theology of Hope* emerges more in an essay in *The Experiment Hope* which introduces *Theology*, than in the volume itself.[40] Be that as it may, the trinitarian conceptuality adumbrated by Moltmann in *The Crucified God* and in later work formed the doctrine of God in a different way, making it a dynamic trinitarianism amounting to a dynamic panentheism. In the era of *Theology of Hope*, there was a clear interest abroad in the connection between a doctrine of God and the future. Harvey Cox, struggling to come to terms with the death of God, announced in his own *Secular City*, admitted that 'if theology can leave behind the God who "is" and begin its work with the God who "will be" . . .' he could get interested in God again: 'An exciting new epoch in theology could begin'.[41] Metz, in his chapter on 'An Eschatological

---

[38] Phan, 'Eschatology', 13.

[39] See her *Sexism and God-Talk* (London: SCM, 1983).

[40] See *The Experiment Hope* (London: SCM, 1975), chap. 4.

[41] Cox, *On Not Leaving it to the Snake* (London: SCM, 1968), 11.

View of the Church and the World', in *Theology of the World*, expressed his preference for translating Exodus 3:14 as 'I will be who I will be'. On this supposition, 'God revealed Himself to Moses more as a power of the future than as being dwelling beyond all history and experience. God is not "above us" but "before us". His transcendence reveals itself as our "absolute future"'.[42] History, in the Son, is 'the actual destiny of the unchanging God'.[43]

The excitement of discovery here is captured all the more effectively for its eager, yet not over-dramatic or uncritical, statement in Schillebeeckx's work, *God—the Future of Man*. Schillebeeckx, pushing *Gaudium et Spes*, agreed that

> the eschatological expectation is not a brake on this building up of a human world, but rather the fulfilment of it by adding new motives; it is a more intensive stimulus towards the building up of the world and this promotion of all nations because the *eschaton* stimulates us to bring about a better earthly future.[44]

He found himself simultaneously moved, as he sought to understand and communicate God in the era of His death, to speak of God as 'our future', the 'wholly New', not 'wholly Other', 'the One who is to come'. Nevertheless, this adds a dimension to God, as it were, rather than providing a wholesale revision; Schillebeeckx was reluctant to let go of the divine presence, so we must think of God as 'our future' without 'overlooking the fact that, according to the Bible, the foundation of the eschatological expectation is the certainty in faith of communion with God here and now'. For 'the foundation of *hope* is *faith* in Yahweh who reveals himself as the living God of the community'. Schillebeeckx held that the neglect of this biblical foundation is an unmistakable drawback in some of the recent 'theologies of hope' and further that 'this neglect fosters an unjustified identification of the promotion of the well-being of all people with the coming of the Kingdom of God'.[45]

Here, too, we must include the massive contribution of Karl Rahner who refused to detach God as Absolute Future from the future of this world and united immanence and transcendence. In Rahner's theology,

---

[42] Metz, *Theology of the World*, 88.

[43] Ibid., 22.

[44] Schillebeeckx, *God—The Future of Man*, 144.

[45] Ibid., 188f.

God is interpreted eschatologically—He is first God of the future rather than present, the 'power of the future', His being intrinsically related to history, His being and actualized sovereignty (that is, His kingdom) one. As Spirit is transcendent in His immanence, so, for us: 'The immanent consummation of a history worked out in freedom by a being endorsed with spiritual faculties is its transcendent consummation because the immanence is its transcendence'.[46]

Finally, we mention another massive contribution, that of Wolfhart Pannenberg. There are features here similar to what we find in Rahner. The end witnesses not only the revelation, but the coming into fulness of God's being; God's future kingdom and future of the world are God's future. At the same time there is, I think, more ambiguity here. The brief communication published as an appendage to Tim Bradshaw's study of *Trinity and Ontology* indicates as succinctly as can be the ambition to maintain the futurity of God's being, not just revelation, but the conceptual formulation of the doctrine seems to me quite unclear.[47] At the same time, a leading conservative and quite sympathetic commentator from the North American continent, Stanley Grenz, finds even panentheism—still more pantheism—'somewhat wide of the mark' in characterizing this position.

> For Pannenberg... God's self-realisation in the world is the revelation in the historical process of the eternal self-realisation present in the inner-trinitarian life... In his understanding the world process does no so much contribute to the reality of God as it reveals what is always present, albeit in a hidden manner, in God's eternity. For Pannenberg, then, God is affected by the world process but not in the sense that this process adds to the divine reality. Rather, the effect of the process lies in the demonstration of the relationship of God over creation, without which God would not be God and cannot be 'all in all'.[48]

Clearly, we should ideally need to probe this further by investigating the semantics of 'lordship' and the relationship between time and eternity which has always had a prominent place in Pannenberg's

---

[46] See Peter Phan, *Eternity in Time: A Study of Karl Rahner's Eschatology* (Selinsgrove: Susquehanna University Press, 1988), 195.

[47] Tim Bradshaw, *Trinity and Ontology: A Comparative Study of the Theologies of Karl Barth and Wolfhart Pannenberg* (Edinburgh: Rutherford House, 1988), 402.

[48] See Grenz, *Reason for Hope*, 211.

thinking. Instead, we take up the reference to 'process', which moves us to a final word on the immediate discussion before we take up the fourth and final section in the wider discussion. Pannenberg has been a natural conversation partner for process thinkers. But a rather distinctive perspective emerges in at least some process thinkers in relation to this-worldly hope. Without regarding all process thought as undifferentiatedly one, let us turn to John Cobb's *Process Theology as Political Theology*.[49]

Spurred on by theology of hope, political theology and liberation theology, Cobb, in 1982, announced his aim of becoming 'a political theologian in the tradition of process theology'.[50] He took up Sölle's phrase 'the indivisible salvation of the whole world' as a guide to the direction political theology should take. For all his support and admiration for political theologians, Cobb, in his very irenic work, warned that 'the conceptual formulations by the three German political theologians [Sölle, Metz and Moltmann] are so vague [on the idea of God] that the consequences could be dangerous for the future of Christian faith in God'. In the case of these three, 'it is hard to determine how seriously we may expect or hope for the promised world. Yet the meaning of hope for us depends on whether it is a real possibility'. Cobb is clear that we cannot confidently anticipate the consummation of the historical process. 'Indeed, history is *really* open'. 'We stand, therefore, before a radically open future with no assurance that our efforts for justice will succeed or even that human history will long continue'. We could well destroy ourselves, so Christian hope 'cannot assure us of the meaningfulness of our actions by pointing towards a future kingdom of God on the planet'. With Whitehead: our resurrection is not on this planet. It is in God.[51]

Two things must be said about this. First, it is clear that we need to go into process thought—more precisely Whitehead's thought—to grasp the full meaning of the claim that our resurrection is in God. Secondly, the commitment to a this-worldly hope is admittedly tenuous here. We certainly need an eschatological basis for socio-political and ecological engagement (Cobb pushed for the inclusion of an ecological dimension

---

[49] J. Cobb, *Process Theology as Political Theology* (Manchester: Manchester University Press, 1982).

[50] Ibid., xi.

[51] Ibid., 71–81.

in political theology), but the eschatological basis is not a dogmatic assertion of divine this-worldly promises. The eschatological basis is God: 'For Whitehead also the eschaton is virtually identified with God'.[52] I think that in terms of our *earth*, the this-worldly/other-worldly option is nugatory; we should have to say that God, a this-worldly entity in His consequent nature, is our hope. We have plenty of incentive for this-worldly commitment; things *may* get better, and that is worth working for.

Now I think that the desire of some process theologians—Brown, Ogden and Cobb—to strengthen liberation, as well as political, theology by giving it a sounder metaphysical basis, indicates an interesting convergence of concerns between process and liberation theologians to which we shall shortly advert. Mention of liberation theology conducts us to our final section, on the question of method.

ESCHATOLOGY AND METHOD

Moltmann's method of deducing eschatological statements can no doubt be variously described, but the christological dialectic of cross and resurrection undoubtedly featured prominently in the early work. Debate over method in relation to eschatology has encompassed many things. Thus perhaps Karl Rahner's best known contribution to eschatology is his discussion of the hermeneutics of eschatological statements, with its anthropological focus and christological control, rejecting any attempt to make eschatological statements descriptions of the future underived theologically from anthropology and christology.[53] Moltmann took a different route: eschatology and christology are correlated by thinking out of the promise, as it were, not by rooting eschatology in a doctrine of the human person, whose fulfilment is attained eschatologically. Pannenberg discovered sharply contrasting approaches here, with promise and anthropology as rivals, but he thought they could be synthesized.[54]

---

[52] Ibid., 78.

[53] Phan, and see Rahner, *Theological Investigations*, Vol. IV (London: Darton, Longman & Todd, 1974), chap. 13.

[54] 'Constructive and Critical Functions', 121.

Rubem Alves, the Protestant liberation theologian, was quite sharply critical of Moltmann in *A Theology of Human Hope*,[55] which appeared not long after *Theology of Hope*. From the outset, we note how differently Alves set about things, beginning with commitment to humanization, elaborating a political humanism and trying to bring the language of promise into this messianic humanism. Hope, the language of political humanism, is from the beginning hope for the qualitatively new and better in history.[56] So how does Moltmann fare?[57] For political humanism 'the transcendent in man is thus deeply rooted in his present . . .'; 'for Moltmann there is no transcendent in the present'. For political humanism 'the powerful present . . . projects itself in the direction of a hopeful future'; for Moltmann it is the transcendent promise that opens up man's future—the present in itself is closed and contains only the possibility of death. For political humanism: 'Man . . . creates the future, which is never determined . . . Moltmann, however, sees the future as already determined'.[58]

When Gutierrez, not long afterwards, came to examine Moltmann, in his classic *A Theology of Liberation*, he overtly supported Alves against Moltmann, but the criticism is far more muted.[59] Gutierrez emphasized single world history, a history of salvation. And the category of Promise is apt: 'The Promise orients all history towards the future . . . Human history is in truth nothing but the slow, uncertain, and surprising fulfilment of the Promise'.[60] Gutierrez cited Moltmann in support here and averred that 'the Bible presents eschatology as the driving force of salvific history radically oriented towards the future. Eschatology is thus not just one more element of Christianity, but the very key to the Christian faith'.[61] This is not explicitly directed against Alves; a kind of middle ground between Moltmann and Alves is potentially in the claim: 'The liberating action of Christ—made man in this history . . .

---

[55] R. A. Alves, *A Theology of Human Hope* (Washington, D.C.: Corpus Books, 1969).

[56] Ibid., 25.

[57] Although Alves also discusses Metz, we restrict ourselves to mention of Moltmann here, as Bonino, whom we discuss below, treats only of Moltmann.

[58] Ibid., 67f.

[59] G. Gutierrez, *A Theology of Liberation* (Maryknoll, NY: Orbis, 1973), 217.

[60] Ibid., 160.

[61] Ibid., 162.

—is at the heart of the historical current of humanity; the struggle for a just society is in its own right very much part of salvation history'.[62] Theology, as a critical reflection on the praxis of liberating struggle, begins with the validity of hopeful human agency. The eschatological kingdom, present in history, transcends limited historical realizations, but historical realizations belong to it, as does human agency, though it is God who ultimately fulfils the transcendent promise.

Much needed to be analysed and clarified here, comprehensively taking in the theme of salvation and liberation.[63] But, to return to Moltmann, the problem, as far as Gutierrez was concerned, was not that he got the wrong end of the stick (Alves' criticism) but that he was one-sided. Moltmann 'has difficulty finding a vocabulary both sufficiently rooted in man's concrete historical experience, in his present of oppression and exploitation, and yet abounding in potentialities . . .'[64] However, it was Bonino's *Doing Theology in a Revolutionary Situation*, published in 1975, that finally provoked a response from Moltmann.[65] Bonino's eschatology does not appear to differ substantially from Gutierrez' in terms of material content. So we can concentrate on his criticism of Moltmann, which was that he failed to relate his eschatological theology to the concrete situation. 'If theology means to take history seriously, it must incorporate . . . a coherent and all-embracing method of sociopolitical analysis. Moltmann does not seem conscious of this need'. He fails to give concrete content to identification with the oppressed. He, with most European theologians, is content to state the critical function of theology 'independent of a structural analysis of reality'. We need more than a new idealism of Christian theology and 'a clear and coherent recognition of historical, analytical and ideological mediation'.[66]

Moltmann's response was instructive.[67] Inasmuch as he engaged in methodological issues, he focused on the use by liberation theologians of

---

[62] Ibid., 168.

[63] See the specific study by Leonardo and Clodovis Boff, *Salvation and Liberation* (Maryknoll, NY: Orbis, 1984). I do not regard liberation theology as a single entity. See J. L. Segundo, 'Two Theologies of Liberation', in A. T. Hennelly, ed., *Liberation Theology: A Documentary History* (Maryknoll, NY: Orbis, 1980).

[64] Gutierrez, *A Theology of Liberation*, 217.

[65] *Revolutionary Theology Comes of Age* (London: SPCK, 1975).

[66] Ibid., 147–149.

[67] 'An Open Letter to Jose Miguez Bonino', in Hennelly, ed., *Liberation Theology*.

European Marxism and of other European thinkers. They stand accused of failing to be authentically Latin American. The hermeneutical question of an engaged reading of texts, clear in Bonino and vital for method, is not touched on, yet it, along with the principle of socio-analysis in theology, was crucial for Bonino's overall argument. What Moltmann did say was that Bonino and his comrades have failed to show how it does not all come out in the wash in exactly the same way as it does in his own theology, when it comes to practical content. For, he averred, scrutiny of the liberation theologians' position reveals that they speak of fragments and anticipations in history, of the kingdom, and not the identification of the historically particular with the eschatologically fulfilled. That is his own position exactly!

His response raises the importance of method. If Moltmann is right, and if, starting from promise, you get where liberation theologians get starting from elsewhere (or elsewhere plus promise) and with different methodological principles, what is the existential importance of methodologically proper procedure here? If the *point* of eschatology is not principally to inform, but is practical, and methodological differences do not generate practical differences, how important is the strife over method?[68] Will not human hope, not just action, phenomenologically shape up in much the same way, whether history is 'broken open' by, for example, incarnation or eschaton? Or are the differences involved really important, registering not here but at another point in theology and practice?

It remains to remark, as promised, on a similarity between process and liberation theologies in this connection. In 1988, Bonino published his essay on 'Love and Social Transformation in Liberation Theology'.[69] Consistent with *Doing Theology in a Revolutionary Situation*, he documented the commitment for change as a work of love. The difference between Latin American and European theology may be quite narrow, but it exists. 'In one case the primary reality is the present awareness of God's love that opens the eyes of hope; in the other, it is the proclamation of the final victory that awakens the commitment to

---

[68] This has interesting ramifications for Moltmann's various treatments of Barth and Bonhoeffer, from whose conceptual schemes he differs somewhat.

[69] In F. Burnham, et al., *Love: The Foundation of Hope: The Theology of Jürgen Moltmann and Elizabeth Moltmann-Wendel* (San Francisco, CA: Harper & Row, 1988).

love'.⁷⁰ Process theology and liberation theology both emphasize divine love and corresponding human love as motivation for action. European theologies frequently seem to require that the motivation be placed in the framework of eschatological hope for the future of this world, and gain strength therefrom.

We are within sight of wide pastures here, and we must stop at the sight. For we should soon stumble upon such things as the dialogue between Moltmann and Brunner which Douglas Schuurman set up.⁷¹ In his *Faith, Hope and Love,* Brunner declared his conviction that love needs no stimulus other than itself.⁷² His work is too early in our century for consideration, but reflection on Schuurman's discussion and on at least some writings in liberation theology provokes the question of whether an emphasis on love in liberation tends first to the demotion, then the marginalization, then the irrelevance of eschatology, for social and political purposes. Indeed, in some modern theology that highlights liberating praxis, it seems to be theologically dispensable.

With these thoughts suspended over us, we are conducted to a concluding reference to feminist theology. In 1975, Letty Russell wrote that 'God's promise leads us to a confidence that the future is open, but not to an exact knowledge of how liberation will be accomplished or what it will look like'.⁷³ She wrote in consistent, though not identical, vein in an essay on 'Authority and Hope in Feminist Theology', published in 1988.⁷⁴

But Ruether, to whom Russell refers in this latter essay, struck a different note. In *Sexism and God-Talk,* this is the problem with historical eschatology. Either (1) 'the end point occurs outside of history altogether and so fails to provide a point of reference for historical hopes' or (2) 'the final era of salvation is identified with a particular social revolution. The

---

⁷⁰ Ibid., 72.

⁷¹ D. Schuurman, *Creation, Eschaton and Ethics: The Ethical Significance of the Creation-Eschaton Relation in the Thought of Emil Brunner and Jürgen Moltmann* (New York: Lang, 1991).

⁷² E. Brunner, *Faith, Hope and Love* (London: Lutterworth, 1957), 57 and see *Eternal Hope* (London: Lutterworth, 1954), 85: 'Whoever lives in the power of love asks no question about meaning because he possesses truth and puts it into effect'.

⁷³ L. Russell in T. McFadden, ed., *Liberation, Revolution and Faith: Theological Perspectives* (New York: Seabury, 1975), 94.

⁷⁴ In Burnham, *Love,* 79.

revolution thereby becomes absolutised'.[75] The moral of this is that we should avoid flight into an unrealized future and concentrate on getting relations just and right on the basis of nature. 'This concept of social change as conversion to the centre, conversion to the earth and to each other, rather than flight into an unrealized future, is a model of change more in keeping with the realities of temporal existence'.[76]

The whole nature of hope-talk changes with God-talk in this enterprise. It takes on different dimensions.[77] Should we connect this with the shift from future to present orientation alluded to earlier? I do not know; the question is somewhat flat-footed. Certainly, however, the story of thirty years of hope can and should be told in tandem with ruminations on justice and on freedom. Gispert-Sauch is surely not untypical, in an account of 'Asian Theology', in stating that any eschatology must be justice eschatology.[78] Alfred Hennelly subtitles his book on *Liberation Theologies*: 'The Global Pursuit of Justice'.[79] As we face the new millennium, there is no doubt that the quest of justice and freedom will go on. The question is whether eschatology will still be part of the universal theological endeavour.[80]

---

[75] See Ruether, *Sexism*, 253.

[76] Ibid., 255.

[77] See J. M. Soskice in T. Elwes, ed., *Women's Voices: Essays in Contemporary Feminist Theology* (London: Marshall Pickering, 1992), 25, where she remarks that she agrees with Ricoeur about religion and hope.

[78] In D. Ford, ed., *The Modern Theologians* (Oxford: Blackwell, 1997), 472ff.

[79] A. T. Hennelly, *Liberation Theologies: The Global Pursuit of Justice* (Mystic, CT: XXIII Publications, 1995).

[80] I have sought to offer critical discussion on some of these topics elsewhere, but I have limited myself here to a descriptive account. Arguably, those who have oriented Christian eschatology to social action, have given hostages to fortune; action can too easily dispense with an eschatological basis. Note that Moltmann, in his most recent work, avoids that pitfall.

II

THE PROBLEM WITH MOLTMANN

Moltmann's work continues to attract a lot of attention. Last year, Richard Bauckham published a second volume on Moltmann's theology.¹ In the previous year, Arne Rasmusson produced the first major study of Stanley Hauerwas' work, in a lengthy comparison of Moltmann and Hauerwas.² This year, Moltmann celebrates his seventieth birthday. This is one reason why the title of this article smacks of the ungenerously churlish. A second is that it is easy to detect problems, compounding the ungenerously churlish with the unduly negative. So, a little compensation is in order on both scores. Firstly, after critical discussion, I shall turn to a constructive proposal. Secondly, and very briefly, I shall try at the end of this piece to locate any elements for such a construction that can be discovered in Moltmann's own work.

WHAT IS THE PROBLEM?

The problem in mind goes a long way back, to the *Theology of Hope* itself. Of course, criticisms of this work also go a long way back and

---

[1] R. Bauckham, *The Theology of Jürgen Moltmann* (Edinburgh: T & T Clark, 1995). His previous work was *Moltmann: Messianic Theology in the Making* (Basingstoke: Marshall Pickering, 1987).

[2] A. Rasmusson, *The Church as Polis* (Lund: Lund University Press, 1994).

Moltmann's thought has gone some way forward in the thirty odd years since it was published. However, the line of criticism I want to pursue here has not been marked out clearly enough, I believe, even in cognate lines of criticism. And although there has been development in Moltmann's theology, there are also constants. Writing, at the beginning of this decade, of his theological career, Moltmann summarized his effort as a reflection on a theology which has: 'a biblical foundation, an eschatological orientation, a political responsibility'.[3] Since then, Moltmann has produced one more volume in a systematic series which began with *The Trinity and the Kingdom of God*, namely *The Spirit of Life*.[4] While he implies that the connections he now makes between pneumatology, christology and eschatology, constitute an advance on *Theology of Hope*, we are not long into the book before realizing that eschatological hope is still to the fore.[5] Pneumatology is treated eschatologically.

So, what is the problem? Moltmann launched his theological campaign in *Theology of Hope* with the claim that Christianity is eschatology. Christology less identifies something thematically distinctive in Christianity than gives particular form to its essential messianism, a messianism which makes it comparable in its intellectual structure to Marxism and to National Socialism.[6] Ideologies that are messianically structured, such as these, owe their existence as this-worldly messianisms to a mistake in the history of Christian thought. What happened was that Christianity lost its true eschatological orientation. It maintained a prominent eschatology, but it was an otherworldly one. So hope for this world emigrated from the church and the church, rather than recapturing its own true eschatological nature, allied its mistaken otherworldliness to a defensive, socially conservative, anti-revolutionary ideology. From *Theology of Hope* onwards, Moltmann has aspired to restore to Christianity its proper dimension of this-worldly hope. This-worldly hope stimulates, drives and gives direction to mission, a mission understood holistically, but distinctively charged by Moltmann with social action on behalf of the poor and the oppressed. Whatever his

---

[3] *History and the Triune God* (London: SCM, 1991), 182.

[4] J. Moltmann, *The Spirit of Life* (London: SCM, 1992).

[5] See, e.g., pp. 7, 69.

[6] 'Political Theology and Political Hermeneutic of the Gospel', 100ff, in *On Human Dignity* (London: SCM, 1984).

tergiversations or expansions, there has been no letup over the course of his authorship in Moltmann's emphases on these points.

So, we repeat, what is the problem? The problem is that the concept of this-worldly hope is troublesome. And the attempts to create an 'ethical field theory for hope', as Douglas Meeks once put it, consequently run into trouble as well.[7] As we examine this concept, we do well to invite our theological consciences to heed words written by Hugo Assmann many years ago. '... Theology is intended as an expression of the hope of liberation, not as a theoretical debate to define hope'.[8] Whether or not this is well said, I shall pick up this point in the course of the discussion.

THIS-WORLDLY HOPE

Why is 'this-worldly hope' troublesome? Because its meaning is unclear. In terms of his overall conceptual scheme, Moltmann has always intended to distinguish between ultimate, eschatological hope and proximate hopes. The former produces the latter. The former is grounded in divine promise. '... The biblical testimonies which it [Christian faith] handed on are yet full to the brim with future hope of a messianic kind for the world ...', declares the opening page of *Theology of Hope*, in which Moltmann begins to unfold the logic of promise.[9] The latter, proximate hopes, are indirectly but not directly grounded in promise. That is, we do not have a promise that proximate realities will turn out well, but we are promised possibilities and, therefore, there is no excuse for despair and every cause for mission. What is possible is derived from what is promised, but is obviously not identical with it. Those who peruse the vocabulary of hope from Moltmann's earliest works will find that it frequently slides without regulation from the one to the other meaning, from a confident, certain hope, correlated to promise, to a hope in the ordinary language sense, where it is contrasted with justifiable certainty. Yet, there is a clear schematic intention to distinguish.

---

[7] M. D. Meeks, *Origins of the Theology of Hope* (Philadelphia: Fortress, 1974), 47ff and 129.

[8] H. Assmann, *A Practical Theology of Liberation* (London: Search Press, 1975), 59ff.

[9] *Theology of Hope* (London: SCM, 1967), 15.

In principle, the distinction between this-worldly and otherworldly hope may be important enough. But there is some question about the way it functions in Moltmann's writing. Moltmann's literature generally exhibits rhetorical indifference to the distinction between 'not x' and 'not only x', but the explicit force of his contention that Christianity has been guilty of an otherworldly instead of a this-worldly hope is obviously lost if the distinction is not in principle clearly maintained. *Prima facie*, the distinction is not a difficult one, and, apparently, only those cursed with the idle theological habit of kicking up dust and complaining that they cannot see, will wonder about it. Yet, the distinction in Moltmann's work is not at all clear, even when we attend to its broad schematic features, instead of focussing on every word, and even when we allow for any positive sense he may ascribe to 'other-worldly' hope.[10] We discover this when we recall a theme which cropped up in his earlier theology and in much theology of that earlier period: the prospect of nuclear disaster. Moltmann's literature has exhibited the wider social shift from nuclear to ecological worry, but the point at issue applies in both cases.

In his work over the years, Moltmann has taken seriously both the extreme nuclear and bleak ecological prospects, which comprehend the devastation of this planet as we know it. He took his time to address these in very specific relation to the theology of hope.[11] But the principle of the problem was taken up in his 'ecological doctrine of creation', *God in Creation*.[12] Here, he rejected the apocalyptic expectation of *annihilatio mundi*, represented in traditional Lutheran dogmatics by Johann Gerhard. He did not deny that the *mundus* could be annihilated. Divine promise is no guarantee against that. To think otherwise would be to refuse to take the nuclear threat seriously. But its apocalyptic *expectation* is a breach of faith in God as Creator. Faith in God as Creator

---

[10] Though the language is short of 'otherworldly hope', note J. M. Bonino's 'Professor Moltmann rightly rejects the dichotomy between a this-worldly (social) and an "other side" (personal) eschatology' ('Love and Social Tranformation in Liberation Theology', 76 n.20, in F. B. Burnham et al., *Love: The Foundation of Hope* (San Francisco: Harper & Row, 1988) and the essay he has especially in mind, Moltmann's 'Love, Death, Eternal Life: The Theology of Hope—The Personal Side', published in the same volume, pp. 3–22).

[11] Richard Bauckham pressed 'theology of hope' on this point in 'Theology after Hiroshima', *Scottish Journal of Theology* 38 (1985): 583–601.

[12] J. Moltmann, *God in Creation* (London: SCM, 1985). Cf. pp. 86–93 and p. 343 n.26ff.

reinforces what Moltmann had long maintained on the basis of divine eschatological promise: whatever befalls, God is committed to the *nova creatio*, the new heaven and the new earth. What Moltmann does not offer is a dogmatic denial of an eschatological *annihilatio mundi* in the name of an alternative *transformatio mundi* as in traditional Reformed dogmatics, as critics from a more conservative wing of the Reformed tradition have pointed out.[13]

Here, then, is our problem. How can we say both (a) that God has given promises for the eschatological future of this world and (b) that this world may be subject to nuclear or other devastation? Moltmann's epistemological moves, from the beginning of *Theology of Hope* onwards, still enable him to join the Christian tradition in placing confidence and having certainty in our hope that God has delivered promises. Hope is not directed to a precarious eschatological possibility. But the prospects for this world are precarious. Moltmann never argued that catastrophic nuclear effects would be limited, in order to suit a theological conviction that this world cannot realize the darkest empirically foreseeable possibilities. Whatever 'this-worldly hope' means, in its ultimate, eschatological nature, it is compatible with nuclear (or other) devastation. Hence my questions. Why should our hope be called 'thisworldly' rather than indeterminate in relation to this world?

One possibility is that, via the notion of 'this-worldly hope', Moltmann is merely insisting on the corporeal and not incorporeal nature of that for which we hope. Corporeality, not continuity, is what matters about the future. This, however, is not a satisfactory response. On a literalistic reading of his work, he does, indeed, maintain the corporeal prospect. But 'this-worldly hope' can hardly mean no more than this. The point may be clearer if we substitute, as Moltmann sometimes does, the phrase 'hope for the historical future' for 'this-worldly hope'.[14] The post-nuclear

---

[13] B.J. Walsh, 'Theology of Hope and the Doctrine of Creation: An Appraisal of Jürgen Moltmann', *Evangelical Quarterly* 59 (1987): 53–76; D.J. Schuurman, 'Creation, Eschaton and Ethics': An Analysis of Theology and Ethics in Jürgen Moltmann', *Calvin Theological Journal* 22 (1987): 42–67; ibid., D.J. Schuurman, *Creation, Eschaton and Ethics: The Ethical Significance of the Creation-Eschaton Relation in the Thought of Emil Brunner and Jürgen Moltmann* (New York: Peter Lang, 1991).

[14] The phrase must be interpreted synecdochically; Moltmann's interest in history expanded to comprehend an interest in nature.

world is surely not the historical future, in the sense Moltmann means that. Of course, if we take Moltmann to be affirming the compatibility of the nuclear prospect with proximate this-worldly hope, there is no inconsistency. But then we are not talking of ultimate eschatological hope, directly grounded in promise.

The difficulties are compounded if we ask what prospects Moltmann has positively held out, over the years, for our historical future. The ultimate eschatological future does not impinge on the proximate historical future just by giving stimulus and direction to our efforts at social change. There are at least two other concepts Moltmann has used to make the connection between the ultimate eschatological and the proximate historical futures. The first, the most pervasive and enduring one in his literature, is the concept of 'anticipation'. In history, while we cannot expect progress until the consummation of the kingdom of God, at least things can happen which anticipate the final outcome. This is a relatively nontechnical notion that emerged not just in Moltmann's thought but on the ecumenical scene more generally, many years ago.[15] The second is 'process'. This one is harder.

'With the resurrection of Christ from the dead and the annihilation of death which takes place through him, the eschatological process of the new creation of all transitory and mortal things begins'.[16] What kind of 'process' is this? The question is the harder to answer because the vocabulary of 'process' was deployed in *Theology of Hope* when Ernst Bloch's conceptualities were particularly prominent. If we need to understand Bloch in order to understand Moltmann, many will conclude that we must penetrate the *obscurum per obscurius*. Without, however, dismissing this possibility, we can certainly note the negative: 'process', in Moltmann, is not 'progress'. The world can get worse, whatever 'tendencies' are set in motion by the resurrection.[17] Moltmann believes this because he believes so strongly in human freedom understood, it would seem, in a libertarian sense. So the 'process' is neither one which definitely prevents the devastation of the earth nor one which prevents

---

[15] See *The Crucified God* (London: SCM, 1974), 287 n.125.

[16] *History and the Triune God*, 78.

[17] The language of 'tendency' is again technical, but more important in *Theology of Hope* (pp. 203ff) than subsequently.

the degeneration of the human lot in history. What, then, is it? It is unclear.[18]

Two objections are possible to the foregoing declaration of difficulties with Moltmann. The first is that it evidences a profound failure of theological imagination, a captivity to a style of theological thought that fails to see the wood of eschatological vision for the trees of conceptual light and shade. In this connection, it may be argued that Scripture itself does not present the kind of description that is apparently demanded in the statement of difficulties with Moltmann. Let it be granted that perhaps a weak theological imagination is culpably contributing to the fact that one is missing what Moltmann is trying to say. Still, he is unclear! On the matter of biblical description, we must remember that nowhere does the Bible pose the 'this-worldly'/'other-worldly' alternative in the conceptually conscious way that Moltmann does, nor speak of a historical 'process' set in motion by promise or resurrection. Those who would go in the name of biblical theology beyond biblical conceptuality, in order to explain its message, are theologically welcome to do so in principle, provided that they explain what they themselves are saying.

A second objection is that our whole dilemma as stated arises from a literalistic reading of Moltmann. It may be argued that Moltmann takes 'this-worldly hope' as a symbol regulating our attitudes towards the world in which we live and move and have our historical being. On this reading, Moltmann means, by his vocabulary, to secure our incorporation into the world of the biblical narrative by using well-grounded theological symbolism which is correlated to desirable types of action. What are we to make of this objection?

We arrive here at what some may regard as the problem area in Moltmann's theology, the subject that really deserves to go under the heading: 'The Problem with Moltmann', namely, the problem of the status of his religious language. Perhaps we are not to anticipate clarification on this point until the production of the final volume in his projected systematics, the volume on theological method. The hermeneutical exercise involved in interpreting Moltmann's language as symbolic would take time and certainly entail a re-description of his

---

[18] According to Richard Bauckham: 'This process is the universal mission of the church', *The Theology of Jürgen Moltmann*, 38. I am not sure that I grasp the meaning of 'is' here. But, as far as I can tell, this interpretation applies 'process' to church, rather than world, history.

claims as I have treated them. But suppose we grant that on the point of 'symbolic', as against 'literal', interpretation of Moltmann, the objection at least presents us with a possible reading. Nevertheless, to cut a long story short, if the symbolism of this-worldly hope is consistent both with the prospect of empirical holocaust and historical decline, it seems to dissociate our historical actions for the proximate future from any connection with what we might meaningfully call 'promise'. And this surely ruptures the fabric of Moltmann's thought.

I am far from claiming that there is no way round the difficulties. There may even be a simple move available to solve our problem, forestalling the need for any conceptual ingenuity. All I claim is that the position is problematic as stated; or, more modestly, that I cannot follow Moltmann's meaning. The same applies if we turn to consider an important feature of this-worldly hope, namely its universalism. By this, I do not refer here to the question of individual human destiny. What is in view is Moltmann's oft-reiterated claim that all reality is destined for eschatological glory. It is spelled out in all its glaring obscurity in *The Way of Jesus Christ*, in the discussion of the 'Eschatological Resurrection of Christ', and especially the remarks on the connection between resurrection and nature.[19] Even Richard Bauckham, a staunch, though not uncritical, advocate of Moltmann's theological enterprise, states that: 'The apparent implication of Moltmann's view that every individual creature that has ever lived—every marigold, every termite, every smallpox virus—will be resurrected in the new creation may seem bizarre . . .' and I do not understand how this problem is eased, as Bauckham says it is.[20] Bauckham's words may indeed confirm the

---

[19] J. Moltmann, *The Way of Jesus Christ* (London: SCM, 1990). Moltmann succeeds in the space of this section in telling us that Christ's resurrection is bodily; that the symbol of the raising of the dead excludes ideas about life after death; that 'all life endures death with pain' (p. 253) and that resurrection has become the universal law for stones (p. 258).

[20] *The Theology of Jürgen Moltmann*, 210: '. . . This problem is alleviated by the novel concept of resurrection which Moltmann introduces in this book. It is that the whole of history (the history of nature and human beings) will be redeemed from evil and death and transformed in the eschatological eternity in which all its times will be simultaneous. So not simply creatures in what they have become in their temporal history, but all creatures as they are diachronically in the process of their history and in all their temporal relationships with other creatures, will be resurrected and transfigured in eternity'. I am unable to understand these sentences.

suspicions of those who hold that my problems with Moltmann stem from a literal or literalistic reading. But then we are back with another set of difficulties in understanding quite what Moltmann is saying. With this, I rest the case for obscurity and submit my problem.

A POSSIBILITY

The problem encountered in the theology of Jürgen Moltmann does, however, generate an interesting and, I think, fruitful theological possibility if we want to essay a constructive response. Suppose that we resist the claim that all individual creatures will be raised or any theological tendency that impels us in that direction. Does it reduce our incentive or imperil our grounds for commitment to the earth? Most of us will say: 'No'. Our hope for what we think of as the cosmic whole does not entail hope for every cosmic particular. In that case, our concern for the particular is not governed by our hope for particulars. The theological basis for concern for the earth can and has been laid out in more or less sophisticated ways, but it is especially pertinent to touch here on the question of love. I may care for the earth out of love for God and for animals. Love governs my relationship to particulars, where eschatological hope does not. Of course, one could elaborate. Eschatological hope may have a role to play in the formation of my love; eschatological hope for the cosmos may have some role to play in the formation of my love for the particular; the nature of love may need logical, phenomenological and theological elaboration to avoid our talk of love being mere truism. Having said all that, love governs particulars where hope does not.

Exactly the same obtains in the case of the eschatological destiny of human beings. Non-universalists will say that we may not hope for the salvation of all, in the sense of entertaining a certain, confident disposition generated by the promise of universal salvation. But they will not say that we can or should not love all. Here, again, love governs the particular where hope does not. (Naturally, we should modify this as we have just done in relation to the earth). Let me assume, at this point, the viability and validity of this position. The question then arises of whether we should deploy the distinction between hope and love in relation to social action, as well, which has always been at the heart of Moltmann's concerns. To put it sharply and at risk of courting an exaggerated response: can we not maintain that our social action is a work of love rather than of hope? If we do so, do we reduce the incentive and imperil the grounds for social action? Certainly, if we do not, the problems with Moltmann's eschatology logically expand into problems with his way of relating eschatology to social action. Let us try to explore the option we have tabled.

LOVE, HOPE AND SOCIAL ACTION

The *prima facie* difficulty with the proposed distinction between hope and love is easy to detect. Apparently, it dissociates loving action from any conviction about human destiny. So it looks as though it fails to regard human beings in an eschatological light. Since eschatological reality is the consummation of salvation and reconciliation, it ousts loving action from a soteriological context. And it is not hard to see where this leads. It creates a dualism: love, impelling social action, pertains to a soteriologically indifferent sphere while hope, which does not govern the particulars of social action, pertains to a soteriological realm, the ultimate-eschatological. Are we not headed for a Lutheran dualism of two kingdoms?

Moltmann has written an interesting essay on Luther's doctrine of the two kingdoms, interesting because he is quite generous in his appraisal, though he is critical. According to Moltmann, because of the brand of apocalyptic dualism which characterizes his theology of history, Luther sees the worldly orders within which one exercises love as orders of preservation, at best, 'but not the anticipatory realization of the kingdom of God on earth'.[21] In this connection: '. . . The two kingdoms doctrine gives no criteria for a specific Christian ethics . . . It is a theology of history but not a foundation for Christian ethics . . . It brings into Christian ethics a realism which reckons with the given facts. But it does not motivate world-transforming hope. That is its weakness'.[22] So an important criterion for Christian ethics is whether it motivates world-transforming hope. Moltmann believes

---

[21] The essay is 'Luther's Doctrine of the Two Kingdoms and its Use Today' in *On Human Dignity*, though I have wandered into a subsequent essay in the same collection ('Political Theology and Political Hermeneutic of the Gospel', 108) to fetch these words.

[22] Op. cit., 76.

that if eschatological hope is a transforming power in history, we have a basis for Christian ethics. (The concepts of ethics and of mission are interwoven in Moltmann's theology, and are interrelated and correlated on a common eschatological basis).

Now Moltmann does not go into the kinds of distinctions between motives and grounds, for example, which would go into a moral-philosophical look at Christian ethics and I shall not seize on the language of 'motive' that he deploys here. But supposing we dwell on Lutheran love. Luther himself has a powerful statement of it in his short Reformation classic, *The Freedom of the Christian*. In it, Luther first expounds justification by faith as a power that transforms the self. But, justified by faith, the Christian is bound to love: indeed, as the believer dwells in Christ by faith, so the believer indwells the neighbour by love. It looks as though, if one took this seriously, one would go a long way in the direction of world-transformation. For if the neighbour labours under oppression of any description, for instance, of a political kind, and if the structure creates the oppression, one is bound to work for its removal. What apparently prevents one from going as far in Lutheran as one can in Reformed theology at this point, is the differing conceptions of government and right of resistance. Just how settled these differences really are, we shall leave open here. But if Lutheran world-transforming action is comparatively limited, its limits do not arise from the logic of love. On the contrary, the love established by Luther as the heart of Christian life, a life justified by faith, seems to strike out in a powerful and positive description towards maximal social transformation.

Still, quite apart from the limits set by a peculiarly Lutheran view of government, is the social dimension of its love so detached from the soteriological issue of history that it reduces motivation to change the world? Emil Brunner remarked aptly on a cognate point forty years ago, though his statements are very succinct. In his discussion of hope, Brunner focussed on Christ as its sole object. Nothing which lacks this object deserves to be called Christian hope. He emphasized that '. . . Christian hope is only that hope for which we have certainty in Jesus Christ himself'. Other hopes, such as the hope of increased justice, are legitimate, even mandatory, but their fruition is not guaranteed. We cannot say of what may happen in history: '*They will occur* [my emphasis] because Christ has come'.²³ Brunner was not arguing that the coming of Christ has no impact on what happens in history. He was refusing to place the object of any particular hope under the constraint of a necessity arising from his coming.

Writing against the background of discussion of belief in progress, Brunner then proceeded to say that one of the fairytales of his age was 'that men need the idea of progress to make them active'. He responded as follows: 'What we really need to make us active is love, and if we have love we need no other stimulus'. We are 'called by Christ to become coworkers with him for the Kingdom of God—and this call is sufficient to activate man's total effort'.²⁴ Brunner gave an eschatological dimension to these remarks in two ways. First, he thought that the hope of eternal life is based on love. Contra Marxism, it follows that it cannot be an opiate, because, based on love, hope of eternal life 'cannot but create love'. Secondly, the hope of eternal life is not just a hope for my destiny. It is a hope for the perfection of the whole of creation, for 'world redemption' and 'world salvation'.

I do not wish to be bound by all the main elements of Brunner's theology at this point, more than by those of Luther. But his stark asseverations throw down a gauntlet. It is hard to add to the motivation of love. How can one limit what it wants to accomplish in this world? It is not dissociated from faith and hope, but it does not need the sphere of its interest to be coterminous with the sphere of hope before it expresses that interest. Indeed, properly speaking, hope applies to the eschatological sphere alone. Now we know that Moltmann admits a distinction of hopes, albeit one that he consistently blurs. But he refuses to distinguish soteriologically and to ascribe salvation to what is ultimate and eschatological, but not to that which is proximate and temporal. Here, he makes a significant criticism of the Reformers. 'The Reformation relativized the political orders, making them necessary orders in this world which can serve the welfare of all, and ought to do so, but do not minister to salvation'. The Reformers made a 'critical distinction between salvation and welfare'.²⁵ The way Moltmann ran

---

²³ For this discussion, see E. Brunner, *Faith, Hope and Love* (London: Lutterworth, 1957), 48–58.

²⁴ Op. cit., 57.

²⁵ J. Moltmann, *The Church in the Power of the Spirit* (London: SCM, 1977), 178.

this argument, found in *The Church in the Power of the Spirit*, is worth looking at more closely.

THE CHURCH IN THE POWER OF THE SPIRIT

In this volume, oriented to the oppressed, Moltmann aimed 'to point away from the pastoral church, that looks after the people, to the people's own communal church among the people'.[26] As the *corpus christianum* decays, the congregation is to press on to 'total testimony of salvation which leaves no sphere of life without hope, from faith to politics, and from politics to economics' (p. 10). This testimony is grounded in the church's comprehension of its commission in world history, 'in the context of God's history' (p. 2), which is more than church history. The testimony is integrated by the conviction that, although liberation takes different forms, 'the freedom that is sought can only be a single and a common freedom. It is the freedom for fellowship with God, man and nature' (p. 17). So: 'Mission embraces all activities that serve to liberate man from his slavery in the presence of the coming God, slavery which extends from economic necessity and God-forsakeness . . .' (p. 10). Again: mission is 'infecting people, whatever their religion, with the spirit of hope, love and responsibility for the world' (p. 152). Although Moltmann might have in principle, and may have in fact, derived this conviction about the unity of freedom from more sources that one, the stated ground of his belief is eschatology. Eschatology is about a single, undivided freedom and our quest for it must be one, its elements (fellowship with God, man and nature) equally weighted. Moltmann has characteristically interpreted the messianic mission of Jesus in eschatological light, a mission which is comprehensive and indivisible. The poor and the captives may be spiritually, physically, socially or politically bound or deprived, but differences of conditions do not allow some kind of hierarchy of liberations. So it is that a true orientation to faith and hope entails rejection of the Reformers' 'critical distinction between salvation and welfare' (p. 178).

Two criticisms of this are in order.

First, the equal soteriological weight attached to diverse forms of liberation cannot be derived from its eschatologically holistic form or

---

[26] Op. cit., xvi. Subsequent page references to this work are given in the text of the article.

nature. The eschatological kingdom may, indeed, be one of personal reconciliation, social freedom and environmental health. It does not follow that there are no pertinent distinctions that apply in the proximate sphere. If the environmental situation deteriorates, we may believe that God will restore it eschatologically; social achievements can be largely undone in time, but we may believe that God will eschatologically establish shalom in its perfection. But what if one's personal relationship to God is marked by increasing indifference, contempt for his law and, bitterness. Is all this eschatologically reversible, no more imperilling our eschatological destiny than environmental disaster imperils the eschatological destiny of the earth? The cases are not the same. That is, the fluctuating conditions of the environment or sociopolitical order do not affect one's entitlement to eschatological hope for 'environment' or 'social order'; but the nature of our personal relationship to God does affect our entitlement to hope for its positive eschatological consummation.

Secondly, let us tritely consider the following. One person is materially poor, educationally disadvantaged, politically deprived—but lives trustingly in God. Another is materially comfortable, free for intellectual self-development, participant in a relatively democratic process, but heedless of God. In biblical perspective, which is nearer to the kingdom of God? To ask the question is to answer it. And to answer it is to distinguish the relationship of different forms of freedom to their eschatological consummation in a way that forces us to differentiate soteriologically between different freedoms. If the New Testament is not telling us that, there is no telling what it is saying.

Of course, no sooner does one say this than the cry of 'dualism' rings through the theological air and all its associated evils crowd to mind. But 'dualism' is not a felicitous word to use for the position being adopted here, particularly if it is a pejorative term. The proper commitment and holistic passion of love in diverse situations is neither compromised nor enervated by the perceived soteriological distinctions. True, soteriological perception will shape one's actions. The relative importance accorded to political liberation and personal reconciliation respectively will doubtless be affected by theological soteriology. Forced, in a particular situation, to choose between time given and importance relatively attached to 'x' and to 'y', one may indeed, on my view, accord less weight to political liberation than to personal reconciliation.[27] But the charge of dualism is in vain here. For the soteriological conviction of those who adopt Moltmann's position must also affect existential priorities in particular cases. Those who, in the name of holism, insist that love of neighbour entails political action, may as easily be accused of existential neglect in the concern for personal reconciliation with God, as often as alleged dualists are accused of existential neglect in their concern for political liberation.

We have framed this discussion by the conviction that love does entail transforming action, and that the loss of Moltmannian hope causes no relinquishment of its proper vigour. I hope, however, that, whatever the truth contained in Hugo Assmann's warning about theoretical debates about hope, its potential practical importance is clear. To proceed further on the trail of praxis, we should need to put particular situations under the microscope—theorizing can appear extremely vacuous otherwise. The meaning of one's theological claims is grasped when one observes how one's language functions in a form of life. I beg the pardon of non-Wittgensteinian readers if this way of putting things complicates life!

MORE POSITIVELY . . .

On the negative side, I have tried to do two things. First, I have quarrelled with the intelligibility of the concept of this-worldliness in Moltmann's theology. Secondly, I have quarrelled with the way he allows hope to govern the grounds for social action. Certainly, we must limit the area of quarrel. On the first point, the argument is not that the claim 'eschatological hope should be this-worldly and not otherworldly' is intrinsically unintelligible or unimportant. I am dealing specifically with the problem in Moltmann's theology. On the second, I am not saying that Christian love is uninformed by eschatological hope. Love and hope are not partitioned absolutely: they are distinguished *ad hoc*. The hopeful passion of love, 'hopeful' in the sense of uncertainty about a particular outcome, can still be fuelled by eschatological hope. Christian life and conviction are deeply disintegrated if there is a move to compartmentalize faith, hope and love.

---

[27] This way of putting matters is shorthand, concessionary and presumes the good will of the reader. I do not assume that 'personal reconciliation' and 'political liberation' constitute some kind of alternative monolithic entities.

Is there anything in Moltmann's thought that is consonant with the proposed emphasis on love? Eight years ago, the proceedings of a conference in the United States, held to celebrate the Moltmanns' sixtieth birthdays, were published under the title of *Love: The Foundation of Hope*.[28] The title refers primarily to divine love, although Douglas Meeks (one of the editors) possibly had human love in mind as well when he wrote that: 'No one in our time has more convincingly shown that love is the foundation, source and power of justice than Jürgen Moltmann' (p. 42). He supports this judgement by reference to the essays collected together under the title *On Human Dignity*. The reference is surprising, not just because Meeks uses such strong language to describe Moltmann's achievement, but because *On Human Dignity* is characteristically dominated by the emphasis on hope, increasingly so as the volume progresses.[29] However, Moltmann does, in this volume, say the following, *inter alia*, about love. In the conclusion to his essay on 'Messianic Atheism', he refers to Dietrich Bonhoeffer on the connection between love of the earth and the resurrection of the dead. Only after one loves may 'one believe in the resurrection of the dead and in a new world'. Moltmann comments:

> There is then no transcending of hope without the paradoxical countermovement of the incarnation of love, no breaking out to new horizons without the sacrifice of life, no anticipating of the future without first investing in it.[30]

This last phrase threatens to scupper a contrast Bonino offered in his contribution to the birthday conference. Here he claimed that while the hope of liberation theologians was awakened by the experience of love in community: 'On the other hand, in European theology, one usually starts with "the promise", a promise that draws "the project" to itself' (p. 72).

---

[28] Op. cit. Page references to this work will now appear in the text of the article.

[29] In this collection, Moltmann contrasts the primacy of love in medieval theology and the primacy of faith in Reformation theology with the primacy of hope, disclosed by modernity and laid upon the theological conscience. Of course, throughout his works, Moltmann gives considerable weight to the importance of love, as well as to hope, in relation to mission and social action.

[30] Op. cit., 186.

At the least, Moltmann's words signal caution in any attempt to schematize his eschatological thinking in relation to life and mission without factoring love into it. I have written this article as though Moltmann were not the author of *The Crucified God*, a theology of love, as well as a theology of hope. It evidences some kinship with the work of Bonhoeffer, whose *Ethics*, to which Moltmann was alluding in the reference above, advances a very powerful christological ground for discipleship, eschatology being present but not dominant.[31] *The Crucified God* was true to its predecessor, *Theology of Hope*, in grounding its christological-eschatological basis for action in crucifixion and not just resurrection.[32] It seems impossible to challenge Moltmann's brand of eschatological theology without attacking the heart of his proposal. But we are talking here about the heart of a conceptual structure. Moltmann's vision of love, and of the way of Jesus Christ, may in some important respects survive criticism. And there, it may be, we shall find the heart of the theologian.

---

[31] If this seems to play down the perceived importance of eschatology in Bonhoeffer's *Ethics*, eschatology nevertheless does not assume the role it assumes in Moltmann's work. Here, Moltmann has been taken as constituting an advance on Bonhoeffer. (See G. C. Chapman, 'Hope and the Ethic of Formation: Moltmann as an Interpreter of Bonhoeffer', *Studies in Religion* 12 (1983): 449–60). Although I shall not argue the point here, I believe that whatever may be gained by strengthening the eschatological element in Bonhoeffer's theology, he grounds our social action more, and not less, effectively than does Moltmann.

[32] 'Christological-eschatological' in that christology is the substance of eschatology in *Theology of Hope*, just as Moltmann's subsequent work is trinitarian eschatology.

III

ESCHATOLOGY AND SOCIAL RESPONSIBILITY: A DEBATE
Stephen N. Williams and Miroslav Volf

THE PARTITION OF LOVE AND HOPE
Stephen N. Williams

One feature of the attempt that has been made for years now to awaken or renew Christian commitment to social responsibility is the interest in eschatology. From the World Council of Churches assembly in Evanston in 1954 the directive went out to probe more thoroughly the relationship of eschatology to social ethics. Evangelicals have also been exploring the links. To many, eschatology is the last thing to turn up for treatment in a book on Christian doctrine; it concerns events at the end of or even beyond the sphere of human history; and it is decidedly the last thing one would expect to influence social ethics. But for a long time now eschatology has been rescued from this fate in varied and prominent theological circles—a welcome fact. Yet some questions need to be asked about the way it is put to work in relation to social responsibility; hence this article. While what follows is largely critical, yet the criticism will give way towards the end of the article to a constructive proposal about the theological foundations of social responsibility. There is certainly no question of denying that eschatological hope shapes all Christian life and conduct. But within the very specific terms of my treatment, the following is proposed: Christian social activity is the work of love, not of hope.

SOME CONTEMPORARY PROPOSALS

Whilst the Grand Rapids consultation on evangelism and social responsibility took place some time ago and discussion has moved on since then, the published papers from it shed a useful light on contemporary proposals to tackle this question, at least in evangelical circles.[1] At least one participant (Peter Kuzmic), in an essay to which we shall return, calls for open, humble, critical dialogue with 'contemporary theologians like Pannenberg, Moltmann and many others, with their stimulating attempts to relate theology to ethics.'[2] Here Kuzmic has in mind especially the connection between eschatology and ethics. For our purposes let us attend to some features of Moltmann's thought in order to lay bare the issue to be addressed. Much water has passed under the bridge since Moltmann wrote *Theology of Hope* over two decades ago, but it still contains his most comprehensive treatment of eschatology to date, and as subsequent modifications in his thought do not affect our present theme, we will briefly revisit it.[3]

Moltmann wanted to give eschatology a new theological centrality and a sounder basis in christology. He also wanted to emphasize that the promises of God to humanity do not refer to some ethereal realm into which the soul may now blissfully escape at death, but to the historical future of mankind. But God intends that His promises for the future bear fruit in world-transforming activity in the present. The resurrection of Jesus Christ opened our world history to a new, transforming power which creates in history anticipations of the promised eschatological destiny.[4] Harnessed to this, Christian social responsibility is a possibility (for hope succeeds despair as the proper Christian attitude to the

---

[1] See Bruce Nicholls, ed., *In Word and Deed* (Exeter: Paternoster, 1985).

[2] P. Kuzmic in Nicholls, op. cit., 'History and Eschatology: Evangelical Views', 155.

[3] For an account of Moltmann's thought up to 1979 see now R. Bauckham, *Moltmann: Messianic Theology in the Making* (London: Marshall Pickering, 1987).

[4] The language of 'anticipation' is often used by others as well as Moltmann, together with words like 'provisional' or 'correspondence' to describe a relation

world) and a necessity (for God wills the eventual transformation of history). This does not mean that Moltmann holds an optimistic view of inevitable progress—far from it. But historical despair is as sinful as pride—often more so.

'THE ESCHATOLOGICAL DESTINY OF MANKIND'

Now we must pause over the phrase 'eschatological destiny of mankind'. It, or some variant on it, is a stock phrase in modern treatments of eschatology. Because God's promises are thoroughly comprehensive, including humanity and the cosmos, so our activity must be comprehensive, excluding no-one and no area. Of the many questions that may arise over the interpretation of this phrase one that naturally comes to mind is whether this implies universalism? Many seem to find this question 'fatiguing': must we really get tied up again, they ask, in questions of who or how many will be saved, when the 'universalism' really worth talking about is something more akin to 'prophetic universalism', the grand vision of God's unlimited future sovereignty now exercised in glorious fullness?[5] It must be granted that we can be unhealthily preoccupied with such a question. But yet we must reflect on it when encountering such phrases as 'hope for all humanity'. Sometimes we use 'hope' in contrast to 'know', as when it is said that we can hope, but not know, that all will be saved. But sometimes, because of the way the Bible often refers to 'hope', we contrast hope to sight, not to knowledge. Hope can be a kind of assurance, not a kind of uncertainty as one usually gets in ordinary language use.

LOVE AND HOPE

Now for those who reject universalism, there are no promises by God to all people in the sense that all will be saved, and hence this is not an object of their hope in what can be called the distinctively theological sense found in the New Testament. (Whether we may 'hope' in the 'ordinary

---

between what can maximally be accomplished in history and what God will establish at its termination.

[5] Guttierez's use of this word doubtless captures the tacit sentiments of many others. *A Theology of Liberation* (Maryknoll, NY: Orbis, 1973), 15, though note the exact context of his use of this word.

language' sense I shall not discuss here though it would be scarcely consistent to do so if one were dogmatically non-universalist.) If hope for humanity is not justified in the sense specified, it cannot, of course, be a basis for mission, including for social responsibility. However, even if there is no biblical mandate that we hope for all, there is every reason to believe we should love all. This introduces us to an important distinction between hope and love, at least for non-universalists. The scope of love is universal; the scope of hope is not. Eschatological hope in this sense cannot be a basis for social responsibility, but love has every possibility of being such a basis. Indeed, one should beware here of artificial distinctions between hope and love—if we had time do so, we could analyze various kinds of hope and the way they well up in the human heart (not just the way they neatly figure on our intellectual register), and various kinds of connections between hope and love. But that should only clarify, not correct, the point being made here. It is a point, however, that should be made if one contemplates dialogue with Moltmann, Pannenberg or others where there is seldom explicit universalism and usually, it appears, an unwillingness to be dogmatic on this question—yet the use of 'hope' in their vocabulary can gloss over important distinctions.

THE CHARACTER OF CHRISTIAN HOPE

An area in which one might expect to find clearer agreement on the part of various theological parties to this general discussion has to do with what we can call the 'this-worldly' character of Christian hope. 'This-worldly' can in fact mean many things, though we tend to treat it as though its meaning were obvious, contrasting it confidently with 'other-worldly' hope. Moltmann's work will again furnish us with an example of the need to define. It is natural and quite in order to say that he emphasizes this-worldly hope as a basis for social responsibility. But by this he does not mean, for instance, that we cannot have a nuclear holocaust which destroys this world in the ways scientists have specified. Nor does he mean that things must get better in this world. He seems to mean both that the future will witness a new heaven and new earth, not a disembodied state, and that the resurrection introduces a this-worldly power.[6]

The question that now surfaces is precisely how such an eschatological outlook is taken to provide us with a superior basis for social responsibility to alternative eschatologies. It is quite possible to hold that our future state will be that of disembodiment and still find compelling reasons for social action. As those who view the future state like that take good care of their bodies, so they might feel compelled by love for God and neighbour to labour incessantly to glorify God, by seeking to conform the world to His will, and to battle incessantly against all that destroys the well-being of their neighbour. Further, it could be emphasized that the Kingdom is present (realised eschatology) and its present form, which is different from its future form, is one where wholeness can to some extent be brought to mind, body, society and environment. In other words, a kind of other-worldly eschatology does not hinder social responsibility, or social action.

Now it may be suspected that all this is playing with ideas. No doubt, it may be said, logically you could have an otherworldly hope and plenty of social drive, though some suspect there is something logically wrong with the connection. But if you do believe that God's future kingdom is a matter of heaven on earth, it will make a difference. Arguments here may range from questions of how historically eschatological attitudes and social responsibility have been related, to questions of how incentives to action are formed at a level which is more psychological than logical, when you bring a certain eschatological outlook to bear on the social task. But an argument which has proved convincing to some, putatively showing that this-worldliness provides a stronger basis for social responsibility than alternative eschatologies, has to do with the continuity between present and future. Indeed, on this issue participants in the Grand Rapids consultation already referred to were divided, yet

---

[6] One certainly should not simply assume that Moltmann is thinking non-symbolically of 'resurrection' either in the case of Jesus or in the future. But if he is inclining to what may be termed a symbolic interpretation of the new heaven and earth it still leads into the kinds of difficulties I am concerned with—perhaps more so.

some insisted that belief in continuity provided an important incentive to social action.[7]

A CLAIM TO ETERNAL SIGNIFICANCE

Peter Kuzmic's paper gave one statement of this position. In it he attacked evangelical withdrawal from the world, one that took its stand on a teaching of total discontinuity, a teaching of an eschatological *creatio ex nihilo* that issues in fatalistic indifference to culture and social involvement. Affirming continuity 'implies that all of our present work for a better world is of eternal significance. It also implies that we are to appreciate and co-operate with non-Christians where in the areas of science, art, literature, philosophy, and social work they are producing what may well be found on the new earth'.[8] As it is shortly after this that he issues the call to dialogue with Moltmann et al., it is worth noting that Moltmann would certainly not put Scripture to the kind of use that has led to such proposals (e.g., in the case of Revelation 21). But leaving Moltmann aside, what are we to make of this claim—one which has, by the way, a plentifully prestigious pedigree in its broad features?

There appear to be several difficulties with his argument. When he claims that discontinuists view the present as 'totally unredeemable' Kuzmic trades on an ambiguity in the word 'redeemable' in this context. Of course, if something does not continue it will not be there to be redeemed. But if 'unredeemable' means 'nothing good or positive can be done with it' then surely Kuzmic is wrong. One can be quite optimistic about what can be achieved in this world without insisting that it continues into the next. Again, as noted earlier, one could hold both to a realised eschatology, with all its implications for prospects for improvement in the world, and to a discontinuous future. However, let us look especially at the claim about producing what may be found on the new earth. That portion of Revelation which speaks of the kings bringing their splendour into the holy city and the glory and honour of the nations appearing there has proved attractive in this context. Perusal of commentaries on this passage, as well as on 2 Peter 3:10 which Kuzmic wishes not to take literally, will show how varied are interpretations

---

[7] J.R.W. Stott, ed., 'Evangelism and Social Responsibility: An Evangelical Commitment' (Exeter: Paternoster, 1982), 41ff.

[8] Op. cit., 151f.

and how insecure is a position which depends heavily on its correct exegesis.[9] Of course, the exegesis of this passage is integrated, by those who think it teaches 'continuity', into broader lines of New Testament interpretation. But what should we make of the claim?

CANDIDATES FOR CONTINUITY

To say that scientific products etc. may be found on the new earth is a trifle ambiguous. It could mean that some such products will be found there but that we do not know which. Or it could mean that some such products just might be found there. In either case one does not know in any given instance whether or not what one is producing has an eschatological future. So at best the incentive seems to be that of a possibility, not that of a promise. But consider the range of things we do or others have done. There are space probes, paintings by Corot, novels by Brontë, social schemes for the rehabilitation of first-time offenders, deeds of mercy towards wounded birds and countless other things ranging from impressive socio-political structures to the casual composition of a limerick. What is or what is not a candidate for continuity? And what does it mean for some of these things to be transformed? Of course, we need not know how God uses these things to believe that He does. But the deeper our agnosticism goes about whether some such products are found on the new earth, and the more we allow that if they are present it is in a radically transformed way, the more we should be inclined to ask whether we are on the right track as regards incentives for social responsibility. Surely all we do is important in God's sight and the least we do or omit to do affects us and others, and what affects us and others we can believe to have eternal significance. But that is not the same as continuity—it could be affirmed by someone who held the future state to be disembodied, or by someone who held it to be embodied but in a totally new creation. Would Bach have had qualms about composing his music if he thought the last we would hear of it would be on this earth? Should structural changes in economics or law to secure animal rights

---

[9] In the New Testament it is only in 2 Peter 3:13 and Revelation 21:1, which of course precedes the verses about the kings (24–26), that one gets talk of the new heaven and earth explicitly, though the phrase recurs in the closing portion of Isaiah in the Old Testament (65:17, 66:22).

or criminal rights be undertaken with an eye on possible eschatological continuity?

THE FUTURE ENVIRONMENT TRANSFORMED OR DISCONTINUED?

It will be observed that the drift of my argument tends not only to challenge continuists but even those who hold firmly that we will be embodied in the future on a new earth, though in discontinuous form in a discontinuous environment. And this indeed is the implication. Let it be clear that I am not denying that biblical eschatology seems to require our emphasizing a form of embodiment and corporeal environment for the future. I am not even denying continuity. It is simply that the form of the eschatological future is, I have argued, a very controversial candidate for the status it often seems to have as a promoter of social action. The fact of the eschatological future may be important here, but form is a different matter. Take the analogy sometimes proposed between resurrection of the body and renewal of the world, alike cases of transformation.[10] All the old arguments about how cremation etc. affects the resurrection of the body here come to mind. Can the world experience nuclear cremation? Whilst the popular idea of what might happen in a holocaust is probably far off the mark, nevertheless scientists are prepared to talk of a process which can be labeled one of eventual extinction of life on earth as we know it. What, then, is meant by denying that 'history and the earth are unimportant spheres destined for extinction'?[11] They are not unimportant, that is true. But what kind of extinction is being denied here? Are we not entitled to say that some things like animals and eco-systems have and may become extinct? What will be transformed and how does the future form have anything to do with the promotion of social responsibility? We are back where we started.

---

[10] It is a familiar one, of course, but see for its use in the context of our discussion C. Sugden and V. Samuel, 'Evangelism and Social Responsibility: A Biblical Study on Priorities' in Nicholls, op. cit., 208ff.

[11] Ibid., 207. Of course, it is hard to know what is meant by history becoming 'extinct' even on principle, unless understood on the lines of extinction when we predicate it of a species of animal, despite the dissimilarities. The whole vocabulary of history 'moving', 'progressing', etc., requires analysis in contemporary eschatological proposals.

Now it is true that we should not ask for greater conceptual clarity than Scripture itself gives us on some matters—that would be a kind of rationalism. But biblical clarity and subsequent theological clarity are not the same thing. Biblical writers did not need to answer some of the questions in the form we ask them, hence they spoke with plenty of clarity for their needs. If, however, one insists on connecting concepts in a way Scripture does not, like eschatology and social action, extra precision is required.[12] Some may say that if our hope clearly is of a corporeal future, or even some continuity in it, it should have some bearing on social action even if we cannot state satisfactorily how—fidelity to the Bible means that we are willing to affirm connections even if we cannot trace them with our logic. But pursuing this would lead us to quite knotty problems about how systems of thought and life interconnect. What seems really questionable to me is, in any case, whether the theological accounts offered, as I have described them, are satisfactory.[13]

In such a brief compass our investigation has been no more than preliminary. That eschatological hope should sustain our social activity is surely right. But even those passages that seem to speak most clearly of renewal rather than complete renovation of the cosmos give us no clue as to how in any particular instance this will apply, and so of any particular work we can but say, at most, that its eschatological transformation is possible. A labour sustained by possibility is not sustained by hope in the theological sense of the word which we have used. In this sense, then, I propose that we do not think of social responsibility as a labour of hope. But earlier we noted the distinction between hope and love. This suggests that we regard our social responsibility as a labour of

---

[12] One can come across text like 1 Corinthians 6:14 where an 'ethical' exhortation seems quite directly linked to the form of the eschatological future. But even if one takes this at face value one has only to consider the kind of entity a 'body' is, compared to that totality we call 'world', to see that its helpfulness as an analogy depends on a rather precise statement as to how the analogy is supposed to work—and this kind of precision is precisely unavailable.

[13] Attention to the contours of Christian life and service, which the logical connection of ideas is often totally incapable of grasping, may certainly show that belief in a disembodied future leads to some surrender of social eagerness. That would certainly matter. Yet the demonstration of this point is not nearly so obvious as some people seem to think, while the social implications of love are, I think, far more obvious.

love, not a labour of hope. Love of God and neighbour remains not just under the law but under grace as the glorious summary of Christian responsibility and nothing we contemplate cannot be included under it. It is, moreover, a mandate of compelling power. The problem with some appeals to love for God is that they are socially quietistic and with appeals to love for neighbour that they merely mean doing one's best on a fairly limited scale—an almost incidental approach to social transformation. That is a total misunderstanding of love. Love for God entails the holy yearning that all in His world should be as He wants it to be. Love for neighbour entails aims to transform structure when victims are not men beaten by thieves on the roadside but men, women and children being oppressed within structures that deny the privileges God means us to have.

Finally, what difference would it make to partition love and hope in this particular respect—and let it be remembered that no absolute distinction is being offered, for along with faith all three should together be thought of as embodied in all we do? Three things can be mentioned. Firstly, it would encourage us to minimize the difference over eschatology that might otherwise occupy us. That is not to propose an eschatological free-for-all; it may well be that certain positions on eschatology will stymie social action. But on questions of this-worldliness and continuity we should relax more, knowing that the mandate for social action is secure.

Secondly, it should encourage us to think more clearly about the relationship of evangelism to social action. By saying that we love a person but may not hope for him in the sense outlined, and that our love for God and neighbour should impel us to socially transforming activity irrespective of eschatological consequences, we distinguish implicitly between the things that do and those which do not make for salvation. To be sure we risk here an artificial dualism. But again it is a question of modifying this perspective as we consider the shape of Christian life, not abandoning it. Jesus' work of healing was certainly part of salvation in a broad sense. Yet surely the compassion which motivated it did not depend on the assurance that eventually it had some sort of eschatological continuation, either in itself or by leading to the spiritual wholeness of the individual.

Thirdly, it encourages us to remember again the majestic supremacy of love in the Christian life. The power of those commandments in the

Pentateuch to love our God and our neighbour should impress itself with no diminution upon us as we progress in the Christian life, longing for the eschatological consummation of all things but unable to discern how our feeble works may be related to it. Love and hope must grow together—but of the bonds that bind them only God can know.[14]

---

[14] In one sense the proposal outlined here is common enough, particularly if one thinks of aspects of mediaeval and Lutheran theology. Exploration of the differences between the understanding outlined above, and mediaeval, Lutheran or Reformed theologies, are beyond our scope here, though it should be obvious that nothing like a quietism is being affirmed! For the record, I stand in the Reformed tradition. I should add in connection with reference to Jesus' work of healing, that one is not here presuming to enter into His inner life and knowledge, but only seeking to reflect theologically on what appear to be the implications of His outward actions.

IV

ESCHATOLOGY AND SOCIAL RESPONSIBILITY: A DEBATE
Stephen N. Williams and Miroslav Volf

ON LOVING WITH HOPE
Miroslav Volf

ESCHATOLOGY AND SOCIAL ETHICS

Christians who want to be faithful to the biblical records do not have a choice whether to construct their social ethic in an eschatological or some other (say protological) framework. The question of how to construe Christian social ethics must be answered within the context of the general discussion of what it means to be a Christian. Moltmann's *Theology of Hope* is right at least in its claim that at the very core, Christian faith is eschatological. Christian life is life in the Spirit of the new creation or it is not Christian life at all. And the Spirit of God should determine the whole life, spiritual as well as secular, of a Christian, and not only some aspects of it. For this reason a Christian's social responsibilities must be carried out under the inspiration of the Spirit and in the light of the coming new creation.

The eschatological nature of Christian existence makes it impossible in my mind to develop a Christian social ethic simply within the framework of the doctrine of creation (protological framework). The new creation is the end of all God's purposes with human beings and with the universe and as such either explicitly or implicitly the necessary criterion of all human action that can be considered good. For God's will revealed to us in Christ is neither particular (only for the church) nor provisional (only for the present world), but universal (for the whole world) and final (for all eternity).

As the resurrection of Christ shows, the new creation does not come about by a negation of the first creation. Rather, the new creation is a reaffirmation of the first. For this reason we cannot exclude the doctrine of creation from our ethical concerns. On the other hand, the new creation is not a mere restoration of the first creation. As O'Donovan has written in his important book, *Resurrection and Moral Order*: 'The redemption of the world, and of mankind, does not serve only to put us back in the Garden of Eden where we began. It leads us on to that further destiny to which, even in the Garden of Eden, we were already directed'.[1] Because the new creation is not a mere restoration of the first creation the doctrine of creation as such is an insufficient basis for developing Christian ethics. It needs to be placed in the broad context of the (partial) realization and of the expectation of the new creation.

ESCHATOLOGICAL CONTINUITY

One can, of course, hold to the view that the new creation is the criterion of all human action and at the same time posit discontinuity between the present and the future world (say by postulating a new creation in the form of disembodied existence in a non-material world). But the belief in eschatological discontinuity is both biblically and theologically unacceptable.

The biblical testimony to the *earthly locale of the kingdom of God* speaks indirectly in favour of the belief in the eschatological transformation of the world rather than its annihilation. As R. H. Gundry has shown, it is 'quite clear that the Book of Revelation promises eternal life on the new earth . . . not ethereal life in the new heaven'.[2] Similarly, in Matthew's

---

[1] O. O'Donovan, *Resurrection and Moral Order: An Outline for Evangelical Ethics* (Leicester: InterVarsity Press; Grand Rapids, MI: Eerdmans, 1986), 55. For the topic of discussion here, the whole chapter 'Eschatology and History' is very instructive.

[2] R. H. Gundry, 'The New Jerusalem: People as Place, not Place for People (Revelation 21:1–22:5)', *NovT* 29 (1987): 254–264, 258.

gospel, the prayer for the coming of the kingdom (6:10) is a prayer for God's 'rule over all the earth' and seeking the kingdom (6:33) 'means desiring the final coming of his rule on earth'.[3] And the 'earth' in the promise of inheriting the earth made to the meek (5:5) can only refer to 'the earthly locale of God's kingdom'.[4]

The stress on the earthly locale of the kingdom of God in the New Testament corresponds not only to the earthly hopes of the Old Testament prophets (cf. Isa. 11:6–10; 65:17–25), but even more significantly to the Christian doctrine of the resurrection of the body. Theologically it makes little sense postulate a non-earthly eschatological existence while believing in the resurrection of the body. The resurrection body demands a corresponding, glorified but nevertheless material environment. Future material existence belongs therefore inalienably to Christian eschatological expectation.

Belief in the earthly locale of the kingdom suggests but does not necessitate continuity between the present and the future orders. One can have a 'this worldly' hope but expect that it will come about through the act of new creation *ex nihilo* rather than through the act of divine transformation of the present creation (so seemingly Moltmann in his *Theology of Hope*). But important and unambiguous New Testament statements (which Williams disregards, mentioning only Rev. 21:24–26) explicitly support the idea of an eschatological transformation of the creation. They indicate that taking the apocalyptic language of the destruction of 'all these things' (2 Pet. 3:11) symbolically might not be merely a matter of individual preference. In Rom. 8:21 Paul writes that the 'creation itself... will be set free from its bondage to decay and obtain the glorious liberty of the children of God'. The liberation of creation—i.e., of the whole of sub-human nature, both animate and inanimate—*cannot occur through its destruction but only through its transformation.* As F.F. Bruce rightly points out, 'If words mean anything, these words of Paul denote not the annihilation of the present material universe of the day of revelation, to be replaced by a universe completely new, but the

---

[3] R. H. Gundry, *Matthew: A Commentary on His Literary and Theological Art* (Grand Rapids, MI: Eerdmans, 1985), 106, 119.

[4] Gundry, *Matthew*, 69. In his article on work in early Christianity Hengel states that a realistic eschatology has its roots 'in the realistic preaching of Jesus and is widespread in early Christianity'. (M. Hengel, 'Die Arbeit im fruhen Christentum', *Theologische Beitrage* 17 (1986): 174–212, 194.

transformation of the present universe so that it will fulfil the purpose for which God created it'.[5]

The biblical affirmations of continuity between the present and future orders are theologically inseparable from the Judeo-Christian belief in the goodness of divine creation (which is a predicate not only of the original but also of the present creation, the reality of evil in it notwithstanding). It makes little sense to affirm the goodness of creation and at the same time expect its eschatological destruction.

According to my reading of the biblical records, we must develop a Christian social ethic within the framework of the belief in eschatological continuity not because of practical (ethical) exigency but because of doctrinal constraints. The claim that we need a particular eschatology for the sake of a desirable social ethics amounts to an illicit functionalizing of theological concepts. We need, of course, to reflect on psychological, social and ecological functions of theological concepts. Their functions, however, may not dictate their content, but the content of theological concepts, formulated in such a way as to take into account their potential misuse, needs to dictate their functions.

ESCHATOLOGICAL CONTINUITY AND SOCIAL INVOLVEMENT

Even if one agrees with the biblical and theological arguments adduced in favour of eschatological continuity, does this belief have any bearing on social and cultural involvement? Williams denies that it does. His argument against the connection between eschatological hope and social action is based less on the belief in discontinuity and more on the following claims: that (1) the belief in discontinuity is at least as good a base for social action as is continuity, and even more significantly, (2) that what we know about continuity is too scant a basis for any kind of informed action.

Williams rightly maintains that it is *logically* compatible to expect annihilation of the world and at the same time strive to improve the life of individual people, to create adequate social structures, and even to be motivated to care effectively for the environment; there is nothing contradictory in wanting to use the world and delight in it as long as it

---

[5] F. F. Bruce, *The Epistle of Paul to the Romans: An Introduction and Commentary* (Grand Rapids, MI: Eerdmans, 1963), 170.

lasts (or as long as human beings last in it). One can consider one's social and ecological involvement as an integral way of loving one's neighbour. For one can believe in annihilation and still affirm enjoyment in this world. The eschatological view that is not compatible with ecological concern is belief in annihilation of the earth combined with the expectation of the immediate coming the Lord. For then one would be wise to reason just as some conservative representative of the Reagan administration did: let us hurry and use up our natural resources for the benefit of human beings before they burn up in a decade or so in a cosmic cataclysm.

Belief in the eschatological annihilation of the world and responsible social involvement are logically compatible. Why then waste time in quarrelling with those who hold to eschatological annihilation instead of simply agreeing to disagree with them, and together getting on with the business of making this world a better place to live? Because belief in eschatological annihilation and social and cultural involvement are *theologically* incompatible. The expectation of the eschatological destruction of the world (and of everything human beings have created in it) is not consonant with belief in the value and goodness of creation: what God will annihilate must be either so bad that it is not possible to redeem it, or so insignificant that it is not worth being redeemed. It is hard to believe in the intrinsic value and goodness of something that God would completely annihilate. The protological belief in the goodness of creation and the eschatological belief in the continuity between present and future creation are inseparably bound together; you cannot have one without the other.

It is, of course, possible to have a merely instrumental view of the goodness of material creation. In that case eschatological annihilation would not deny the goodness of creation. Like food, all other material objects are good because they are necessary for keeping the human body alive, and the human body is good merely because it provides a temporary dwelling place for the soul. At another level, material creation can be seen as merely instrumentally good since one can consider it a temporary means of manifesting God's greatness and glory. I would not want to deny or denigrate the instrumental goodness of the material creation. But I would want to insist that the material creation is not merely a means but is also an end in itself precisely because the doctrine of eschatological continuity gives it 'soteriological independence':

creation too will participate in the liberty of the children of God (cf. Rom. 8:21). And according to my theological anthropology, human beings do not only have a body, but they also are a body. The body is not simply an instrument but an integral part of their identity as particular human beings. Hence the goodness of the human body is intrinsic, not merely instrumental.

The main point here is that *without a theologically grounded belief in the intrinsic value and goodness of creation, positive cultural involvement hangs theologically in the air.* Hence Christians who await the destruction of the world (and refuse to live a conveniently schizophrenic life) as a rule—out of theological not logical consistency—shy away from social and cultural involvement. The only theologically plausible justification for cultural involvement, under the presupposition that the world is not intrinsically good, would be that it diminishes the suffering of the body and contributes to the good of the soul (either by making possible evangelism or by fostering sanctification). Bodily pleasure— say, enjoying a beautiful sculpture—could have no more positive value in and of itself than does the body itself; it could be merely a means to some spiritual end. This, however, is not the case if one believes in the intrinsic goodness of creation, and one can believe in the intrinsic value of creation only if one believes in the eschatological transformation rather than destruction.

What about Bach? If he were an annihilationist, should he have had qualms about composing music? Not necessarily. He could have seen his music as one way of loving his neighbours—who happen to be spiritually elevated by listening to his music—and in this way glorifying God. (Under annihilationist presuppositions Bach's music could not have glorified God directly because it would not have had any intrinsic value. Only the sensation of pleasantness based on a temporary arrangement of matter in the form of human hearing organs would make Bach's organ music more beautiful and valuable than is the sound of my fingers hitting the computer keyboard.) Bach, however, would have had little theological reason to compose his music simply because he wanted people to take pleasure in it.

The ascription of intrinsic value and of ultimate significance to positive cultural involvement is not the only benefit of developing a theology of work within the framework of belief in eschatological continuity. In addition, such belief gives human beings important inspiration for cultural, social and ecological action even when such action is not appreciated by one's neighbours. How often they do not appreciate one's efforts at doing good deeds, at finding the truth about some aspect of reality, at creating beauty! The question is not merely whether Bach would have reason to compose his music if he were an annihilationist. The question is also whether all those unappreciated small and great van Gogh's in various fields of human activity would not draw inspiration and strength from the belief that their noble efforts are not lost, that everything good, true and beautiful they create is appreciated by God and will be appreciated by human beings in a new creation.

After I have affirmed the importance of eschatological continuity for an adequate theological grounding of cultural, social and ecological action, I should issue a call to realism. The question whether Bach should have had qualms about composing his music if he thought the last we would hear of it would be on this earth, presupposes that people work *because* of their belief in eschatological continuity. But for the most part they do not. Neither do they work *because* they want to love their neighbour. Most of us work because we have to survive or because we want to succeed. Hunger and pride are the main incentives for human work. I have little reason to think that our sermons (and even less our theological reflection) will significantly alter this state of affairs. The call to love our neighbour and our belief in eschatological continuity will produce not so much a change in the inner motivation of our work (although this too will, hopefully, sometimes happen), as assurance and inspiration, and provide the criterion for judging the results of our work.[6]

ESCHATOLOGICAL CONTINUITY—HOW SHOULD WE THINK OF IT?

How should we think of the continuity between the results of our social and cultural work and the eschatological future? Is it not contradictory to ascribe eternal permanence to what corruptible human beings create? A chair gets broken in a year, bread eaten in a day, and a speech forgotten

---

[6] I believe that human achievements do not lose their inherent value because they were done out of ethically impure motives. Every noble result of human work is ultimately significant.

in an hour. Most of the results of human work will waste away before they see the day of their eschatological transformation. What about the eschatological destiny of 'space probes, impressionistic paintings by Corot, novels by Bronte, social schemes for rehabilitation of first-time offenders, deeds of mercy towards wounded birds and countless other things ranging from impressive socio-political structures to the casual composition of a limerick' (Williams)?

When we think about eschatological continuity, we should not think only in terms of the work of isolated individuals, but also of the cumulative work of the whole human race. The work of each individual contributes to the 'project' in which the human race is involved. As one generation stands on the shoulders of another, so the accomplishments of each generation build upon those of the previous one. What has wasted away or been destroyed often functions as a ladder which, after use, can be pushed aside. Second, although on the one hand, much of human work serves for sustenance and its results disappear almost as soon as they have appeared, on the other hand, much human work leaves a permanent imprint on the natural and social environment and creates a home for human beings without which they could not exist as human beings. Even if every single human product throughout history will not be integrated into the world to come, this worldly home of human beings as a whole will be integrated.

Third, work and its perceived results define in part the structure of human beings' personality, their identity. Since resurrection will not be a negation but an affirmation of human earthly identity, and since what will be resurrected will not simply be a human being in the state in which he or she existed at the point of death, but the whole life of that person (it will occur diachronically),[7] earthly work will have an influence on resurrected personality. Would Gutemberg in a glorified state be Gutemberg apart from any eschatological relation to the discovery that made him famous? Would all human beings who have benefited from Gutemberg's discovery in their glorified state be themselves without his discovery? Human work is ultimately significant not only because it contributes to the future environment of human beings (cosmological

---

[7] For this view of resurrection cf. J. Moltmann, *Der Weg Jesu Christi. Christologie in messianischen Dimensionen* (Munchen: Chr. Kaiser, 1989), 285ff.

level), but also because it leaves an indelible imprint on their personalities (anthropological level).[8]

It could be argued that one could affirm the anthropological level of the eschatological significance of human work even if one held to the annihilation of the world. Strictly speaking this is true. But it seems inconsistent to hold that human creations are evil or insignificant enough to necessitate their destruction and that their influence on human personality—which should be carefully distinguished from the influence which the process of work has on an individual's sanctification—is good and valuable enough to require eschatological preservation.

THE FACT AND THE FORM OF THE ESCHATOLOGICAL FUTURE

Williams admits that 'the fact of the eschatological future may be important' as a promoter of social action. He claims that 'eschatological hope should sustain our social activity'. But how should eschatological hope do that? The eschatological future does not bear upon present action only with its promises of reward and threats of punishment for deeds done in this life. The fact of eschatological continuity—even if we do not know precisely what will be preserved eschatologically—indicates that mundane work has significance beyond the well being of the worker, his community and posterity. It guarantees that noble human efforts will not be wasted. After having been purified in the eschatological *transformatio mundi*, the results of human work will be integrated by divine action into the new heaven and the new earth. Through their work, human beings contribute in their modest and broken way to God's new creation.

Christian hope gives not only inspiration but also direction to cultural, social and ecological involvement. This is where Williams and I might disagree. He claims that 'the *form* of the eschatological future is . . . a very controversial candidate for the status it seems often to have as a promoter of social action'. In a sense, this is correct. For we do not know precisely what form the eschatological future will take and are hence ignorant as to which particular results of human work will

---

[8] Similarly, recently: 'The Oxford Declaration on Christian Faith and Economics', *Transformation* 2 (1990), para. 18.

be preserved. Yet, *do we not know what kind of work will be preserved*? It will be work which was done according to the will of God. Like gold, silver and precious stones (cf. 1 Cor. 3:12) such work will survive the fire of God's judgment, purified. But like wood, hay and straw, the work which was done against God's will will burn up, for 'nothing unclean will enter' the new creation (Rev. 21:27).

The ultimate significance of work done according to God's will brings us back to Williams' main concern: preservation of the 'majestic supremacy of love in Christian life'. For what is the will of God for which we will no longer have to pray to be done in the new creation? It is God's commandment of love (accompanied with the demand to seek after truth and beauty). So love is the key for the anticipatory discernment of how our feeble works are related to the eschatological consummation of all things. We should, therefore, resist the partition of hope and love.

Williams' suggestion that we base social action on love rather than on hope makes sense only if we first empty Christian hope of love and make Christian love into a non-eschatological reality. But we can do neither because love has 'been poured into our hearts through [the eschatological gift of] the Holy Spirit' (Rom. 5:5). God who 'has spoken to us in these last days by His Son, whom He appointed the heir of all things, through whom also He created the world' (Heb. 1:2), revealed something of how love and hope must grow together: the practice of love is an integral part of the content of this-worldly eschatological hope; and the object of eschatological hope is the fulfilment of the dreams of love.[9]

---

[9] I would like to thank Judith Gundry Volf for her critical interaction during the writing of this article. It was composed in my spare time as a Humboldt fellow in Tübingen.

V

ESCHATOLOGY AND SOCIAL RESPONSIBILITY: A DEBATE
Stephen N. Williams and Miroslav Volf

EVANGELICALS AND ESCHATOLOGY: A CONTENTIOUS CASE

Stephen N. Williams

David Wright outstandingly combines scholarship, churchmanship and evangelical commitment. Amongst his longstanding concerns, and one close to his heart, is the social dimension of Christian witness and endeavour. Back in 1979, he edited papers from the significant National Evangelical Conference on Social Ethics, held in the previous year.[1] His continued commitment to the matters which occupied him there was indicated in a powerful editorial in the *Scottish Bulletin of Evangelical Theology*.

'... How commonly', he asked, 'does the designation "Calvinist" imply for the modern evangelical in Scotland the particular theological perspective which most obviously distinguished the Reformed from

---

[1] D. F. Wright, ed., *Essays in Evangelical Social Ethics* (Exeter: Paternoster, 1979).

other varieties of sixteenth century Protestantism? This was, of course, the vision of the godly ordering of the whole of society. It is likely to be a poor history of the Reformation that fails to single out the shaping of the total life of the community according to the will of God as perhaps the most distinctive mark of Calvinism'.[2]

He proceeded to lament (i) *'the paucity of evangelical contributions on the broad front of Christian socio-political responsibility'*; (ii) *'our non-involvement with wider evangelical developments in this field'*; (iii) *'the inadequacy of our common evangelical "line" on socio-political issues'*.

He made brief, but valuable, proposals for remedying this deficiency. But I shall not follow here the trajectory of these proposals. Rather, I shall use as a springboard his remarks under the second of the points above. The 'wider evangelical developments' which he instantiated here were those embodied in the Lausanne Covenant. In particular, he cited the Grand Rapids consultation, held under the aegis of the Lausanne movement and the World Evangelical Fellowship, in 1982. The report came out later that year, and Bruce Nicholls edited the papers published three years later.[3]

I make no apology for revisiting these documents twelve to fifteen years on. It is surprising how little progress has been made in some evangelical circles since then, in key areas of this discussion.[4] Our quarry in this essay is just one of the issues, namely, the relation of eschatology to social responsibility. More specifically, we are interested in the bearing of our beliefs about the relation between the present and the future on our social engagement. Although the brief labours that follow are expended mostly on clearing ground and blocking off routes, it is in the hope that the high road of social action be traversed with as little impediment, and as much confidence, as theology can contribute.

---

[2] 'Rediscovering a (Scottish) Evangelical Heritage', *SBET* 4 (1986).

[3] John Stott chaired the drafting committee of the report, entitled *Evangelism and Social Responsibility: An Evangelical Commitment* (Exeter: Paternoster, 1982). Bruce Nicholls edited the papers entitled *In Word and Deed: Evangelism and Social Responsibility* (Exeter: Paternoster, 1985).

[4] This was particularly impressed on me at a conference last year where some of the Lausanne issues were re-run in a company where one would not expect it. And this was no isolated instance.

THE QUESTION OF CONTINUITY

At Grand Rapids, intra-evangelical disagreements surfaced in relation to eschatology.[5] There is one point in his report on the consultation where John Stott noted inability to agree. This was in the area of eschatology. Representatives of the three millennarian positions (amillennialism, premillennialism and post-millennialism) at the consultation had no desire to address those differences directly. But while there was common ground on the matter of 'eschatological motivation for evangelism and social responsibility' (p. 38), the question of whether 'the final Kingdom [will] enjoy some continuity with its present manifestation', or whether 'the future [will] be discontinuous with the present...' evoked disagreement (p. 40). The disagreement bore on social action. 'Those who have the assurance of this continuity find in it a strong incentive to social and cultural involvement' (p. 42).

The force of this disagreement emerged when the consultation papers were eventually published. 'History and Eschatology' had occupied a day of the discussion and Peter Kuzmic's paper, in particular, focused the issue that will interest us.[6] But the issue came up in other papers. Its importance, and the significance of Kuzmic's subsequent contribution, were stated early and clearly in David Bosch's paper, where he described premillennialism as a negative influence on social involvement, a trend that had hindered understanding.[7] We will concentrate on what Kuzmic said.

When Peter Kuzmic laid out the three main options on the millennial question, he expended by far the most time on premillennialism. This was on account of its supposedly deleterious social consequences. On the one hand, he granted that 'there are varieties of premillennialism leading to significantly varied practical and behavioural consequences' (p. 141). But he took it that 'premillennialism's underlying philosophy of history has almost inevitable negative consequences for Christian social responsibility', citing Donald Dayton and Timothy Weber

---

[5] For the context of the consultation, see p. 9 of the report. Page numbers to various works will occasionally be placed in the text of this essay, where it is clear which work is cited.

[6] Peter Kuzmic, 'History and Eschatology: Evangelical Views' in *Word and Deed*.

[7] David J. Bosch, 'In Search of a New Evangelical Understanding' in *Word and Deed*, 71ff.

in support (pp. 142–44). On this view, only when Christ returns are there decent prospects for the earth; evangelism is our task until then. Kuzmic protested against this purely futuristic eschatology and neglect of the reality of the Kingdom already come, whose blessings are meant to include social blessings.

Tied to the neglect of realised eschatology is the emphasis on a 'radical break between the present earth and the awaited "new heaven and earth." Such teaching of total discontinuity sees the present completely unredeemable and under judgement of divine destruction, and the "new earth" to be a kind of a new *creatio ex nihilo*' (p. 151). And so, as well as affirming realised eschatology, Kuzmic affirmed a continuity between this earth and the next, without denying discontinuity. 'We are to work for a better world already here and now, knowing that everything that is noble, beautiful, true and righteous in this world will somehow be preserved and perfected in the new world to come' (p. 151). In his support, he cited those who stand in the Dutch Calvinist tradition (Berkouwer, Berkhof and Hoekema) and Calvin himself. He concluded by pressing for a connection between eschatology and ethics, whereby both the presence of the Kingdom and the promise of its consummation in some continuity with this earth would ground, or help to ground, our social as well as our personal ethics.

I shall not pursue the case against premillennialism here. But let us look at the case for continuity. It is particularly interesting to notice the role played, in recent evangelical debate, by a text Kuzmic highlighted in support of his position, namely, Revelation 21:24–26. We encounter this text more than once in this collection, e.g., in the contribution by Vinay Samuel and Chris Sugden.[8] They, too, embed reference to the text in a wider argument for continuity, on the analogy of the resurrection of the body. The practical consequence of this latter belief is that we must deal with people here and now according to their bodily reality, according to the 'series of integrated relationships' in which we live. They press on as follows. 'Such an understanding of transformation equally applies to our stewardship of creation . . . . All the Old Testament concepts of the Kingdom of God are in terms of a renewed earth' (p. 209). One conclusion is that the values expressed in 'good works performed within

---

[8] See Vinay Samuel and Chris Sugden, 'Evangelism and Social Responsibility: A Biblical Study on Priorities' in *Word and Deed,* 209, though they refer strictly to Revelation 21:22–24.

the structural relationships of human history . . . are heavenly values which will last forever. So too the works which express these values inasmuch as they belong to the new age, will find their fulfilment in that age' (p. 210). So Kuzmic is not a voice crying in the wilderness. But there are difficulties.[9]

DIFFICULTIES

The prominence given, in recent years, to Revelation 21:24–26, is rather curious. Anything approaching exegetical consensus on this text, either within or without the evangelical community, is unlikely in the near future. Not that this should preclude staunch advocacy of a particular option. Nor that we should throw up our hands in hermeneutical despair. It is just that we are on precarious ground.

A number of commentators affirm in general that Revelation 21 teaches the continuity of the new with the present heaven and earth, albeit in transformed mode, and they affirm in particular the support Revelation 21:24–26 gives to this standpoint. But the contrasting approaches can be illustrated by three examples chosen from the decade or so before the Grand Rapids conference.

Leon Morris took John to be 'concerned with spiritual states, not with physical realities', his description of 'a complete transformation of all things' making use of 'the language of heaven and earth for he has no other language'.[10] He had earlier glossed 'there was found no place for them' (i.e., earth and sky, or earth and heaven, Rev. 20:11) as meaning 'they were completely destroyed'. He found the bringing of the glory and honour of the nations into the new Jerusalem (21:26) hard to understand. Shortly afterwards, George Eldon Ladd, in his commentary on Revelation, argued that the element of discontinuity was stronger in the New than in the Old Testament, as exemplified by the closing

---

[9] There is a number which I shall not pursue here, e.g., the analogy with the resurrection of the body is difficult to sustain effectively. The person and the body are relatively simple compared to the heterogeneous mass of things that constitute 'the world'. Another issue is the semantics and significance of the linguistic distinction between two Greek words for 'new', *kainos* and *neos*.

[10] Leon Morris, *The Revelation of St. John: An Introduction and Commentary* (London: Tyndale, 1969), 242f.

chapters of Revelation.[11] On 21:1, he observed: 'The abolition of the sea suggests that there is practically no substantial continuity between the old fallen and the new redeemed order, but that the old order is completely swept away and replaced by something altogether new and different'. True, 21:5 'suggests the renovation of what already exists. But it is improbable that the apocalyptist was much concerned about such details; his attention is fixed on the coming of the new order'. Finally, we refer to Robert Mounce's commentary published in 1977.[12] He concluded that neither the language of 21:1 nor rabbinic commentary enabled us to decide between 'renovation of the old or a distinctly new creation'. On 21:24, he remarked that the 'imagery of the Apocalypse must of necessity be concrete and spatial, but its significance is inevitably spiritual'.

I am not expressing agreement or disagreement with anything in these comments. But they indicate the controversial nature of appealing to Revelation. However, the difficulty is compounded—and it is this that constitutes the main difficulty, in our present context—when the application of Revelation 21:24–26 is made in detail. Consider these words of Hoekema, to whose work Kuzmic appealed.

> Whatever people have done on this earth which glorified God will be remembered in the life to come (Rev. 14:13). But more must be said. Is it too much to say that, according to these verses, the unique contributions of each nation to the life of the present earth will enrich the life of the new earth? Shall we than perhaps inherit the best products of culture and art which this earth has produced?[13]

The questions are rhetorical, expecting respectively negative and affirmative answers. Having cited Hoekema, Kuzmic affirmed that 'we are to appreciate and co-operate with non-Christians where in the areas of science, art, literature, philosophy, and social work they are producing what may well be found on the new earth' (p. 152).

---

[11] G. E. Ladd, *A Commentary on the Revelation of John* (Grand Rapids: Eerdmans, 1972), 271ff.

[12] Robert H. Mounce, *The Book of Revelation* (Grand Rapids: Eerdmans, 1977). Note that references in my essay are deliberately not to commentaries written post-Grand Rapids, for I am not entering the exegetical arena directly.

[13] A. Hoekema, *The Bible and the Future* (Exeter: Paternoster, 1979), 286.

To parrot Hoekema: is it too much to ask what we mean here? Transformed Constables? Revised Brontés? Reconstructed *Summae Theologiae*? And what about the mass of our social work, geared towards containing social problems? Now some may get impatient with such questions and argue as follows. Scripture is not in the business of, and theology has no responsibility for, such specific description. If one pursues my line of questioning, with its uneasy hint of mockery, one may be found in contempt of God himself, who bids us believe in continuity and transformation, but not on the strength of our ability to conceptualise. It would be a truly fatal attitude to Scripture and to the whole theological task if statements of faith were subjected to this kind of demand for conceptual precision.

Such a demurral contains much that is serious, valuable and true. But it does not detract from the force of our questions. For talk of literature, art and science is introduced not by Scripture, but by advocates of continuity. Such specificity is the alleged entailment of a theologically sensitive exegesis of Scripture, which provides an incentive for action. The Christian effort in literature, art, science, philosophy and social work, and the Christian appreciation of non-Christian literature, art, science, philosophy and social work, is enhanced by such a reading of Scripture. So it is claimed.

However, the claim is deeply problematic. It raises the question of whether works which, it may be conceded, are perhaps not destined for such a specific form of consummation, somehow lack a motivational dimension that the others possess; of whether Christians engaged in art, innocent of the potential eschatological destiny of their products, lack the motivational edge possessed by the continuists.[14] We can extend the line of questioning beyond examples principally from the world of human commerce and human artifacts. When the 'continuism' which surfaced at Grand Rapids was challenged in an article in *Transformation*, in 1990, Miroslav Volf offered a rebuttal on behalf of the continuist

---

[14] It is worth scrutinizing interpretations of the disappearance of the sea (Rev. 21:1), to see if they have any logical bearing on our present responsibilities towards the marine environment. The discussion usually carried on does not go in for distinctions between motives, incentives, grounds, reasons etc. So I am using the word 'motive' very loosely.

position.¹⁵ According to Volf, 'important and unambiguous New Testament statements . . . explicitly support the idea of an eschatological transformation of the creation'. This is not based just on a text from Revelation. The text Volf himself took up was Romans 8:21, where Paul refers to the liberation of creation. Citing F.F. Bruce in his support, Volf commented: 'The liberation of creation—i.e., of the whole of sub-human nature, both animate and inanimate—*cannot occur through its destruction but only through its transformation*' (p. 29). As heretofore, transformation and continuity are mutually implicative notions. But does the turn to Romans help?

The fact is that Bruce's own formulation is open to serious questioning, when he requires that we interpret the apocalyptic language of Revelation via these 'more prosaic statements'.¹⁶ The loose comparative in this claim is a stumbling-block when one considers the insistence of a C.H. Dodd, for instance, that this language is 'poetic' and 'as little as possible dependent on any particular metaphysic'.¹⁷ However, we need not at all enlist Dodd to make the point that counts here. Volf's emphatic reference to 'the *whole* of sub-human nature' indicates equally emphatically the problem with his own position. For what about the animals? Volf seems committed not only to the position that there will be animals on the new earth. He seems committed to the belief that these will be transformed animals from the present earth, and the prospect of transformed particular animals—not just those of the last generation—is meant to furnish some kind of incentive for caring for them. Is this *reductio ad absurdum* not just the logic of Volf's own insistence?

It is intriguing to watch Charles Hodge in action on this passage. Hodge was a robust transformationist, arguing the Reformed position against Lutheran annihilationist interpretations of the future of the universe.¹⁸ In his commentary on Romans, he interprets 8:21–25 along

---

[15] M. Volf, 'On Loving with Hope: Eschatology and Social Responsibility', *Transformation* (7.3) 1990. He was replying to my article, 'The Partition of Love and Hope: Eschatology and Social Responsibility', in the same issue.

[16] F.F. Bruce, *The Epistle of Paul to the Romans: An Introduction and Commentary* (London: Tyndale, 1963), 170, n.2.

[17] C.H. Dodd, *The Epistle of Paul to the Romans* (London: Hodder & Stoughton, 1932), 132f.

[18] Charles Hodge, *Systematic Theology* (New York: Scribner, 1873), 3:851–855.

similar lines, although he does not shrink from insisting on Paul's poetical vein. It may be thought that he ducks the question about animals that arises from his own interpretation of the creation (*ktisis*) that is to enjoy eschatological liberty. But he does make the programmatic assertion, in a sentence picked up by John Murray in his later commentary, that the words 'the whole creation' are 'so comprehensive, that nothing should be excluded which the nature of the subject and the context do not show cannot be embraced within their scope'.[19] 'The nature of the subject', in addition to 'context', invites pause. The issue before is not whether Scripture speaks of the eschatological transformation, as opposed to the annihilation, of the present cosmos. The issue is what continuity can be inferred from transformation; how alleged continuity constitutes the destiny of particulars; and how or whether our perception of the destiny of particulars affects our treatment of them. In addressing this further, we now need to chart rather deeper and wider theological waters.

DEEPER REACHES

Volf's riposte to the criticism of continuism was vigorous. He went beyond reference to Romans and to exegesis. He agreed that although one could logically marry a contrary conviction, one that maintained discontinuity, with social action yet, theologically, there are insuperable difficulties. The central one is this: 'The expectation of the eschatological destruction of the world (and of everything human beings have created in it) is not consonant with belief in the value and goodness of creation: what God will annihilate must either be so bad that it is not possible to redeem it, or so insignificant that it is not worth being redeemed. It is hard to believe in the intrinsic value of goodness of something that God would completely annihilate'. Thus, 'one can believe in the intrinsic goodness of creation only if one believes in eschatological transformation rather than destruction' (p. 30).

This argument, however, gets into serious difficulty if it is offered, as it is, from within an evangelical perspective. This is clear when we consider the question of universalism. What is of most value, what is the pinnacle of goodness in God's creation? Humanity. Yet, on the non-universalist view, some humans reap destruction. Supposing

---

[19] Charles Hodge, *Commentary on the Epistle to the Romans* (Edinburgh: Andrew Eliot/James Thin, 1875), 268.

one synecdochically substituted that which is of greatest importance in the world (humanity) for 'the world' in the sentence quoted from Volf. Then it reads: 'The expectation of the eschatological destruction of the human being . . . is not consonant with belief in the value and goodness of creation'. That spells universalism. One presumes that, on Volf's wording, it is immaterial whether one believes in annihilation or in everlasting punishment. In either case, the supremely valuable is not redeemed. Yet, the fact is that the desperate eschatological destiny of part of the human race does not mean that it initially lacked created goodness or value. Then, *a fortiori*, why should putative destruction be inconsistent with goodness and value in the case of 'the world'?

Of course, there is a ready answer to all this. Some humans eventually go beyond redemption. Humans may be destroyed when and because they allow their inherent goodness and valuableness to be negated by sinfulness. Participation in a fallen world does not disqualify from redemption, but responsibly sinning within it does. But if Volf's position is something like this, note that the implication of his reasoning is not just the negative—that the participation of the good and the valuable in the fallen world does not disqualify it from redemption. It is the positive— what is created good and of value thereby qualifies for eschatological redemption. Which surely means that all the hamsters that ever were will be transformed eschatologically, their annihilated non-appearance being inconsistent with their created goodness. More: this fact gives us an additional incentive to comb out the hair of the loosehaired variety, lest the tangles cause consternation.

I do not mean to trivialise in any way. Hamsters are not insignificant. It is part of the greatness of God that not a hamster feels pain, discomfort or consternation without our heavenly father knowing and caring. But there is something important at stake here: the bearing of eschatological hope on the particulars of social action which concretely constitute our earthly responsibility. It is as though the more specific or concrete our asseverations on eschatological hope, the more we have the problem of relating that hope to earthly particulars in the way under scrutiny. Now there is a wider problem here, not confined to the form in which we have encountered it in the Lausanne context. We find Volf, in his essay, appealing to Oliver O'Donovan's treatment of 'Eschatology and

History' in *Resurrection and Moral Order*.[20] Here, as we might expect, theological reasons for belief in transformation, are lodged within a firm conceptual structure. We turn to it at this juncture, because it broadens our enquiry out of its original context in the Lausanne debates, while keeping us close to the biblical material.

O'Donovan's treatment turns out to be problematic along lines that we can identify from our enquiry. Introducing his general thesis, he argues that the resurrection of Christ is theologically central for ethics, since 'it tells us of God's vindication of his creation and so of our created life'. He adds that 1 Peter is 'the most consistently theological New Testament treatise on ethics'. Its great declaration of living hope through the resurrection 'proclaims the reality of the new life upon which the very possibility of ethics depends' (p. 13). A second reference to 1 Peter, in Part One of the work, conducts to its conclusion the argument that 'Christian ethics, like the resurrection, looks both backwards and forwards, to the origin and to the end of the created order. It respects the natural structures of life in the world, while looking forward to their transformation' (p. 58). All this is exemplified in 1 Peter, which opens with a declaration of hope, and moves on to such things as ethics of government, labour and marriage. O'Donovan avers that 'a hope which envisages the transformation of existing natural structures cannot consistently attack or repudiate those structures', though the institutions need redemption.

The transformation envisioned here is eschatological, including a comprehensive dimension of future redemption. But again the Bible is unconvincingly used in the advancement of a theological thesis about transformation, which logically seems to entail some form of continuity, although O'Donovan does not commit himself here. For nothing in Petrine hope clearly envisages such an eschatological transformation; the question of eschatological transformation is, as far as this letter goes, irrelevant to Peter. Even after investigating the Jewish background to 1 Peter, to see whether Petrine hope is really as otherworldly as it *prima facie* appears, the epistle meets with stony silence any who would enquire, on its basis, and with deep theological intent, whether natural institutions are to be abolished or transformed. Nothing in resurrection hope shapes its ethics in that particular respect.

---

[20] Oliver O'Donovan, *Resurrection and Moral Order: An Outline for Evangelical Ethics* (Leicester: Apollos, 1994).

O'Donovan does, of course, seek a broader biblical basis for his theological ethics than what he finds in 1 Peter. He may object that Petrine hope must be assimilated to wider New Testament hope; when it is so assimilated, we can read into the logic of Petrine hope an entailment as to the transformation of natural structures. The *locus classicus* is Romans 8. O'Donovan speaks of transformation here, when God redeems the whole of creation, which must, as a whole, fulfil a God-given purpose. '. . . This fulfilment is what is implied when we speak of the "transformation" of the created order' (p. 55). '. . .We must understand "creation" not merely as the raw material out of which the world as we know it is composed, but as the order and coherence in which it is composed' (p. 31). 'Creation is the given totality of order which forms the presupposition of historical existence. "Created order" is that which neither the terrors of chance nor the ingenuity of art can overthrow' (p. 61).

We quote these words to indicate O'Donovan's emphasis, which runs out (as far as it interests us) in the conviction that Petrine and more generally biblical natural structures of natural life in this world, qua part of the created order, must be destined for eschatological transformation. It is important to remember that, while O'Donovan steers studiously clear of having transformation entail the kind of strong continuities we have encountered, his 'fulfilment' is opposed to eschatological annihilation.

However, the language of 'wholeness' or 'totality', while aptly characterising biblical eschatological promises *per se,* hinders, rather than helps, when pressed into the service of grounding ethics, in the mode that we are encountering here. O'Donovan consistently refers to the eschatological destiny of humankind, treating humanity as a 'whole'. Yet, he appears to reject universal salvation. So the humanity to whom a glorious destiny is promised is not the sum total of all individuals. On the meaning of redemption for the non-human creation, he professes agnosticism but, obviously, when one considers botanical or zoological natural *history,* sum total, again, is scarcely an option.

'Natural structures' or 'institutions' are not the same as either people or biological organisms. How should we take them as some sort of whole, in some kind of generic solidarity? What could it mean to say that they are destined for transformation, by virtue of their participation in a larger whole? One thinks of legal structures (more exactly, perhaps, logical provision for justice), generically a feature of political society as God has established it in this world, the promotion of justice being a central biblical theme. It is only at a stratospheric level or generalization that one could insist that we must term what happens to them 'transformation' rather than 'abolition'; indeed, one might deny the right to do so at all. The claim that there is some sort of wholeness to creation destined for transformation, according to biblical witness, is compatible with agnosticism on the question of whether the massive natural structures which we indwell have any kind of eschatological future.

Ex professo, O'Donovan's motive for retaining 'transformation' language is, in the first place, the preservation of whatever Scripture means when speaking of *fulfilment* in the eschaton. But on that score we must say this: in Scripture we are summoned to live our lives on this earth in relation to a host of things that may simply, like heaven and earth, 'pass away'.[21] Our behaviour in their regard is not characteristically governed by our perception of their destiny, and the onus is on those who are theologically reflective about it to specify in some detail why the theological logic of biblical eschatology leads us to insist on transformation and on its importance in relation to specific moral conduct. The eschatological status of the structures and institutions in question is so opaque that it is hard to see how the conviction that there is a whole to be redeemed affects our ethics within them. A response to some of these charges is not difficult to anticipate (though I shall not rehearse it), but it seems to me that an unsatisfactory unclarity remains. Our difficulties with eschatological wholes and earthly particulars surely remain.

CAUTION

In drawing to a conclusion I want to be very cautious about the direction of my own argument and a trifle non-committal on its conclusions. For until one has come to terms with the powerful tradition of Dutch Calvinism on the pertinent questions, one ought to suspend judgement.[22]

---

[21] With this reference, I am not committing myself to any particular exegesis of Matthew 24:35.

[22] Douglas Schuurman noted some of the sources here in *Creation, Eschaton and Ethics: The Ethical Significance of the Creation-Eschaton Relation in the Thought of Emil*

Those of us who cannot manage Dutch are debarred from access to the crucial theological contributions of Abraham Kuyper on this point, not to mention those of others in his tradition. Kuyper has invested this tradition with such weight that those of us who are linguistically below par ought to keep an open mind on the subject that has detained us. Still, I want to advert briefly to two who stand in that tradition: G. C. Berkouwer and Hendrikus Berkhof.[23] My self-imposed caution is partially, though not entirely, matched by an element of caution in these authors too, which we ought to notice.

Berkouwer, despite compelling reservations about the terms on which Reformed theologians of eschatological transformation argued their case against the Lutheran theology of annihilation in the seventeenth century, clearly throws in his lot with the former.[24] Faced with the choice of Thurneysen's highly concrete description of continuity and Brunner's rejection of its dogmatic content, he opts for the first. Against Brunner's superficially laudable agnostic restraint, Berkouwer says: 'If he is completely correct about this, why do the Old and New Testaments not talk about an "x"—an unknown quantity—instead of arousing these various concepts of what the new heaven and the new earth will be like and talking about the longing for the creation for freedom from its perishability? The need for sobriety in talking about these matters ought not to lead one to overlook the equal need for certainty' (p. 232). 'If he is completely correct' indicates a note of restraint in Berkouwer's dissent from the position he rejects. Still, caution is tempered by conviction.

Brunner and Jürgen Moltmann (New York: Peter Lang, 1991), 157, n.12.

[23] Both Kuzmic and Hoekema appealed to these two. I do not deny the appealing nature of the position which I am challenging, as found in work which lacks hermeneutical discussion, like that of Richard Mouw, especially *When the Kings Come Marching In* (Grand Rapids: Eerdmans, 1983).

[24] G.C. Berkouwer, *The Return of Christ* (Grand Rapids: Eerdmans, 1972), 219ff. This was translated and edited from the Dutch original. Reference to the seventeenth century debate allows us to make a point which is also relevant to Volf's strictures against those who *expect* cosmic annihilation. Note how Moltmann, in his opposition to the Lutheran tradition, seems not to deny the *possibility* of annihilation, only its positive *expectation*. See Moltmann, *God in Creation* (London: SCM, 1985), 86–93. The latter signifies an attitude to Creator and creation not necessitated by the former. I may be misinterpreting Moltmann here, but I assume that his point is that expecting is very different from permitting annihilation.

Without prejudice to Berkouwer's wider discussion on these points, it should be pointed out that there are two difficulties attached to the formulation quoted. First, the New Testament *does* sometimes point to an unknown 'x'.[25] Second, we encounter here an hermeneutical question about eschatological statements, unaddressed at this point, which also needs more thorough attention in contemporary evangelicalism. The question we ask of Berkouwer is this. If what is to be transcends our ability to conceive it, what words should be used to describe it? What compelling objection is there if Scripture were held to take the finest that we can imagine, stating its eschatological message of wonderful consummation in those terms, as a substitute for stating an abstraction that signifies our lack of knowledge? Is that so foreign to the way that the language and imagery of the Bible works?[26]

Our second figure, Berkhof, is rightly prepared at least to cast a peripheral glance in the direction of this question at this point, briefly discussing the relationship of faith to imagination, in *The Christian Faith*.[27] In this work, Berkhof seems to modify or to qualify tacitly, but significantly, the 'continuist' position taken in an earlier and well-known work, *Christ, the Meaning of History*.[28] In *The Christian Faith* Berkhof will not be dogmatically forced into a choice between these following possibilities.

> We can say that our culture provides the scaffolding for the coming structure, a scaffolding that will later be torn down again. It is also possible, however, to view our culture as providing the building materials for a coming kingdom.

---

[25] I am thinking here less of the extent to which individual texts, like 1 John 3:2, might be pressed in the service of such a claim, than of a sustained discussion such as 1 Corinthians 15.35ff. I cannot exegete that here, but it seems to me that attention to the logic of the argument, and the distinction between *sarx* and *sōma*, even in the wider Pauline context, warrants our description of the spiritual body as an unknown 'x'. However, I believe that this should be qualified by, and is consistent with, a credal affirmation of the resurrection of the body. It would take too long to say how and why!

[26] The phrase is borrowed from G. B. Caird, *The Language and Imagery of the Bible* (London: Duckworth, 1980), whose third part treats eschatology.

[27] H. Berkhof, *Christian Faith: An Introduction to the Study of the Faith* (Grand Rapids: Eerdmans, 1979), 539. But see n.34 in chapter 1 of the present volume.

[28] See the third edition of this (London: SCM, 1966). Note also a brief study: H. Berkhof, *Well-Founded Hope* (Richmond: John Knox, 1969).

He settles finally for 'the fact that all of cultural development will prove to be meaningful in the light of eternity. But that is the limit of what can be said about eternity' (p. 539). That is a good way short of the strong continuism which launched our investigation in this essay. Berkhof is not remote from the following conviction, although he does not sanction it: while the prospect of continuity appears rich, if it turns out in the eschaton that we have made over-literal deductions from the biblical data, we shall certainly not be disappointed or feel impoverished. The eschatological scene will strike us in all its transcendent majesty. How can it not, when God will be all in all?

CONCLUSION

> Hear O Israel, the Lord our God is one. Love the Lord your God will all your heart and with all your soul and with all your mind and with all your strength. This is the first and greatest commandment. And the second is like it: Love your neighbour as yourself.[29]

These non-identical but twin commandments are set in the realm of grace, in Old Testament as in New. The whole of the Christian life of faith and of love is set in the light of hope.[30] One cannot conceive of Christians engaging in social action detached from an eschatological context. But neither can one conceive of a limit to what the love of God and neighbour should, and should desire to, accomplish—a limit, for example, set by the possibility of non-continuity between present and future. Such is the nature, power and mandate of love that it demands great rigour on the part of the proponents of transformation and continuity, versus annihilation and discontinuity, to demonstrate that their incentive is *required* by full-orbed biblical Christianity in order to undertake our social responsibilities to the greater glory of God. My own conviction, for what it is worth and which I shall not elaborate here, is that the mandate for social responsibility is adequately secured

---

[29] I am conflating the Matthean and Markan renderings of the great commandment here.

[30] Col. 1:5 refers to 'the faith and love that spring from the hope . . .' although this is not a standard way of relating the triumvirate.

by love, within a more general eschatological framework than our continuists allow.[31]

David Wright may not welcome, and may dissent from, the tentative conclusion of this essay. What he will undoubtedly welcome is the suggestion that the matter would be profitably pursued by continued enquiry about the theological basis of the Reformers' theology of social concern, a matter he brought to light in the *SBET* editorial with which we started. Indeed, he has led the way in the matter. He edited *Martin Bucer: Reforming Church and Community* to mark the quincentenary of Bucer's birth.[32] Of his subject, he said: 'It would be difficult to find a sixteenth-century churchman and theologian with more say to the churches of Europe now living through the disorienting transition between the old order of the Christian establishment and the emergent ex-Christian (rather than post-Christian) pluralistic world' (p. 2). Although neither David Wright nor his fellow-essayists pursue Bucer's theology of society and action in connection with his eschatology, we should learn much from Bucer, as from other Reformers, of that passion which drives the true believer to care for God's world, and of the theological sources of that passion.[33] It will all be found to be of such power and profundity that although it may please God that we grow in theological insight as the centuries pass, yet if we perch ourselves on these giant shoulders, we shall have ascended high indeed. It is no wonder that David Wright has recalled us to the Reformation. It is not the least of his contributions to have summoned us to consider our social responsibility in its light. May our deeds, not our theology alone, be enriched by his reminder.[34]

---

[31] I certainly do not mean that anything goes in eschatology. For example, I fully agree with emphasizing the 'now' of the Kingdom.

[32] D. F. Wright, ed., *Martin Bucer: Reforming Church and Community* (Cambridge: Cambridge University Press, 1994).

[33] The first two essays in this volume on Bucer indicate what we might mine: P. Matheson, 'Martin Bucer and the Old Church' and M. Greschat, 'The Relation Between Church and Civil Community in Bucer's Reforming Work'.

[34] In 1956 T. F. Torrance wrote on 'The Eschatology of Love: Martin Butzer', in *Kingdom and Church: A Study in the Theology of the Reformation* (Edinburgh: Oliver & Boyd, 1956). He noted Bucer's comment on the Isaianic reference to the new heavens and new earth, which is '*magis de Ecclesiae innovatione et foelicitate spirituali, quam de futuro mundi statu, immutationeque corporali*' (p. 88). But Torrance's comparative studies in this study and the work on Bucer now in progress deserve careful study by those interested in the theological and eschatological foundations of social concern.

VI

THE LIMITS OF HOPE AND THE LOGIC OF LOVE
On the Basis of Christian Social Responsibility

It has long been said that social action is the offspring of love but by now we are also familiar with the claim of hope to conjoint parental rights and responsibilities. To propose that hope has determinate limits with regard to social action looks like playing Canute with the contemporary theological tide. The story is often told of how scholarship appeared to secure for eschatology its place in the New Testament a few decades ago at the cost of uprooting it from any stable home in dogmatic theology. But its odyssey ended with the discovery of a congenial partner, viz., social action and since the 1960s we have witnessed a brood of theologies proficially spawned, mandating socially transforming activity partly or largely on the basis of eschatological hope. That is the background to this lecture whose focus, none the less, is biblical rather than dogmatic. The following is a proposal that we distinguish between love and hope in relation to social responsibility and action without suggesting a schism designed to spice up in unsanctified fashion the theological task.

Reference to biblical, as opposed to dogmatic theology, requires comment. All the distinction states is that we are asking about biblical perspectives and not taking on the dogmatic task of asking about the status of such perspectives in relation to the contemporary theological endeavour. But 'biblical perspectives' also requires comment. The deliberate design of taking broad biblical themes in the compass of a single lecture obviously risks first, imposing artificial unity on the material and secondly, neglecting exegesis. This warning is well taken and, I hope, heeded. If distinctions are not explicitly made and exegesis is not explicitly offered I hope it will at least be clear that care has been taken to propound a thesis that is fully alert to the relevant range of questions. Having said that, it is as well to let the kind of argument presented show forth its contours in the actual presentation, or the *qui s'excuse s'accuse* syndrome which hovers over introductory remarks will be in too much evidence.

In his *Biblical Ethics and Social Change*, Stephen Mott provides us with a comprehensive and focused discussion of principles of biblical theology of social action.[1] We begin by being parasitic on this account particularly as it embodies the kind of plausible and solid conclusions that will strike many as evidently correct. While he adopts as an overall perspective the cosmic conflict with evil, Mott finds the direct biblical mandate for social action rather 'in the models associated with God's activity in the world than the theology of the cosmos' (19). Four themes emerge. First there is grace, grounding all Christian ethics, its bearing on social responsibility clarified as it shades into the second theme of love. Though the author speaks of the third theme, justice, as providing 'the most direct and far-reaching biblical authorization for social action' (77), justice is a form of love. The relations of love to justice are variously described. Justice may complete the work of love or be its instrument, carry out its implications or be transcended by it. Justice is the social incarnation of love (hence we may call it a 'form' of it). All this is argued exegetically. Supremely, when we read the New Testament love commandment in the light of the Old Testament motif of social justice, we have the firmest of biblical grounds for a theology of social involvement.

Eschatology is the fourth theme. The broad idea is that 'the Reign of God is a central biblical concept which incorporates the imperative for social responsibility into God's goals for history' (82). Keeping again the Old Testament background in view Mott emphasizes both realized

---

[1] (Oxford: Oxford University Press, 1982).

and future eschatologies. Now, with Jesus, the divine reign makes its incursion into the world, including its sociality; then, in future, God will triumph on the cosmic scale. History presses on to this goal. The power within and the promise before history thus constitute an imperative for socially transforming activity. We shall not follow Mott's development of this line. Rather, we focus on a problematic feature in his discussion. This has to do with the relation of the grand totalities of consummated history to the several particulars of social endeavour. The following phrases and claims quoted from his work are chosen not just to cite his words but because they ring familiar and seem conceptually innocuous.

Speaking eschatologically, 'all will join in the song of Revelation (90; cf. Rev. 11:17); 'Christ's work affects all of history' (95); 'the ultimate purpose in history is the total sovereignty of God over all things' (101); 'in the end all the created world—people, supernatural powers, natural forces and institutions—will be conformed to the will of God' (101). The scene is cosmic and universal. So what of the relation of the eschatological future to present activity? Not only does hope embody values which we must pursue but 'the demand of God upon us now is intensified by anticipation of the future' (91); our small victories 'speak of the approaching outcome', our historical struggles are 'not irrelevant to the coming of God's full reign' (96); 'the effort to build a temporal city is relevant to the divine work of redemption' (103). But there is a deeper strand. Mott grants that 'God is not asking us to build eternal structures but to accept our responsibility for God's creation' (91) but he also speaks of God as 'creating and building up His reign' (106), of the last events as being under way and of the conquest of evil as being 'in process' (95). However, let us select the following assertion as a springboard for discussion: God's purpose in the present age is 'to narrow the gap until Christ not only reigns but assumes complete control of the governments of the world' (90).

'Narrowing the gap' is a picture and Wittgenstein graphically illustrates how we can be misled by pictures in our thinking.[2] Of course the question of the relation of pictorial representation to conceptual thought is an old one. In the field of New Testament studies, modern discussion got its distinctive stimulus from the work of D.F. Strauss,

---

[2] Norman Malcolm, *Ludwing Wittgenstein: A Memoir* (Oxford: Oxford University Press, 1958), 53f.

its background including Hegel's attempt to translate religious images into philosophical concepts. In our century it is above all Amos Wilder who put together the issues of eschatology and social ethics, picture and concept in New Testament scholarship, and his concerns are still alive. There is a cluster of issues involved here but we must stick to one question: what is being conceived of when we hear talk of 'narrowing the gap'? The biblical narrative may indeed encourage us to picture history as moving forward to its destiny, a grand totality heading for eschatological consummation. Now if that is the narrowing of the gap, the gap is chronological. But there is another gap: the qualitative one. On a theory of progress, the gap is narrowing too. But Mott is not committed to that theory.[3] What, then, does he take to be a biblical perspective on qualitative improvement in history? Let us assume there are criteria for improvement. Presumably Mott allows that deterioration as well as improvement marks history before the eschaton. So what is meant by 'narrowing the gap'? Is it just a chronological truism? Or, if it is a qualitative concept, does the gap widen in some ways and narrow in others? Or is there a distinction between God's purposes and God's accomplishments? We are not told.

Possibly it is the failure to reflect on the relation of pictures to concepts in adumbrating a biblical theology that lies behind Mott's conviction that Rauschenbusch clinched the argument for the pursuit of social righteousness.[4] According to Rauschenbusch the argument that we postpone striving for social righteousness on the ground that we cannot achieve it until the eschaton is doomed for the simple reason that such an argument should prevent us from pursuing personal holiness as well. But the argument fails to note the distinction in the way present and future are related in the respective cases. Those who do not grow in holiness, who do not seek to narrow the gap between what they are and what they will be, risk forfeiting the destiny for which they hope, for spiritual progress in this life is in some measure a ground for entitlement to hope for perfection in the next. Even those who argue for universalism on a biblical basis may want to affirm some version of that claim. However, God's promise of a new heaven and new earth is not related in the same way to cosmic progress; it stands for the world

---

[3] Though see an unexplained phrase in 'The Use of the Bible in Social Ethics' in *Transformation* 1.3 (1984): 21: 'a tendency toward change'.

[4] Mott, *Biblical Ethics and Social Change*, 91.

even if the world degenerates until the eschaton. Mott certainly along with the majority of biblical scholars, seems to hold that the realization of the eschaton is not contingent on overall progress. So the cases are not parallel.

The question is, then: what does the biblical sense of a grand totality really contribute to the social imperative? Can what God 'creates', 'builds' in history be torn down in history? Can states of affairs which seem to anticipate the eschaton mutate into states qualitatively at odds with the eschatological prospect? If deterioration is possible, how is the relation between eschatological fulfillment and temporal accomplishment to be described? No attempts will be made here to answer all questions but they are generated by any who formulate as does Mott a basis in biblical eschatology for social responsibility.

It is unquestionably true that New Testament materials (on which we concentrate) present us with scenes of the cosmic or universal scope of redemption, even if the propriety of phrases sometimes used (like 'redemption of all history' or 'redemption of institutions') are not to be taken for granted where biblical linguistic usage is concerned. Romans 8, the opening chapter of Ephesians and of Colossians, Revelation 21 or notions like *apokatastasis* and *paliggenesia* are standardly cited in this connection. Yet what kind of totality or comprehensiveness is involved in such passages or concepts? The debate over universalism, still occasionally rumbling on in New Testament studies, helps us here. According to nonuniversalists, eschatological totalities are not sum totalities: any talk of 'all humankind' is not talk of all humans where inclusion in salvation is under consideration. A grand totality, in such an analysis, is not every particular.

On any reading of the passage cited, to take eschatological wholeness as a totality of particulars is futile. Romans 8:18ff. furnishes us with an example. There is a strong case for reading *ktisis* here as a reference to non-human creation.[5] According to a 'strong' reading of this passage we should include within the sphere of redemption here everything not obviously or explicitly excluded.[6] Even here, however, a sum total is scarcely in mind. For that would include all animals and all trees. Such

---

[5] Even Käsemann so interprets it; see *Commentary on Romans* (London: SCM, 1980), ad loc.

[6] See, e.g., John Murray, *The Epistle to the Romans* (Grand Rapids, MI: Eerdmans 1967), ad loc.

an argument applies *a fortiori* to those who interpret Revelation 21:24–6 as implying that all that is best in human culture will be preserved in the eschatological kingdom. It applies *a fortiori* just because there is far less exegetical consensus for such an interpretation than there is for reading *ktisis* here as a reference to non-human creation, and that is because the argument concerning *ktisis* is basically linguistic (though context and genre are relevant) while the argument concerning the passage from Revelation is more broadly hermeneutical. However, even granting the possibility of the above interpretation of the entry of the kings, the scope of this passage in relation to the particulars that constitute human culture can obviously only be stated in the most general possible way. It is true that interpreters of passages such as the above are well aware of the difficulty of trying to net biblical talk of the transformed eschatological order in empirically-based concepts. It is true that such passages do not gain their force from their attempted application to all the particulars of history. Nevertheless our line of inquiry is neither banal nor inconsequential. What is its significance?

The significance is that it posts a warning about our use of the concept 'hope' when we relate eschatological hope to social responsibility. When a non-universalist speaks of 'hope for all humanity' he does not mean 'hope for all humans' in the sense that eschatological promises of salvation apply to all particular individuals. Even universalists will not mean by 'hope for history' or for 'all creation' or for 'the whole world' promises for all particulars. In an important sense, then, 'hope' does not govern our relationship to all particulars. Of course, the word does not bear a single standard meaning in the Greek New Testament. But it is sufficient for our purposes to pick out a use of it typical of Pauline and Petrine literature and of the letter to the Hebrews where it is explicitly or implicitly correlated to divine promises.[7] Of course one may describe Christian existence in the New Testament as eschatological existence and even argue that future hope in vast tracts of its literature governs our attitude to all life, including, therefore, every particular person, event and activity. But that is not the same as hope (in the sense under consideration) on behalf of all particulars. Particular temporal events may occasionally be governed by divine promise in Scripture. But there is a distinction between eschatological promises and what constitute

---

[7] Of course, *elpis* can be the substantive object, not just the subjective attitude.

from the human point of view a seething mass of possibilities in the minutiae of human life.

The statement of all this has twofold significance in the present context. First, in contemporary biblical and dogmatic theology the vocabulary of hope in relation to social action is marshalled under the banner of the eschaton without consistently distinguishing between the promised and the temporally particular. Even when a point is technically correct, 'hope' slithers around uncomfortably. To cite one exegete notably attentive to language:

> These days we have reduced the blazing certainty that the New Testament calls hope to a cautious optimism that fits these uncertain times. This is an unfortunate situation, because hope is vital. Has any truly effective social or religious movement—one that really gripped people—failed to inspire hope in its followers?[8]

But what is the 'hope' of a social or religious movement hope for? If it is a blazing certainty of success in the venture it is unwarranted without special divine revelation. Leon Morris' subsequent remarks on slaves, outcasts and women reveal that the point he makes is consistent and true enough, but what he leaves unclear is the relation between the hope *embodied* in a social or religious movement and hope *for* that movement.

Secondly, the preceding discussion opens the way for formulating a thesis about social action. Mott gave pride of place to love (and justice), not eschatology. With regard to hope we pressed the question of the relation of the eschatological whole to the temporal particular. Love seems to govern the particular in a way different from that of hope. A non-universalist does not hope for all in the sense of 'hope' which interests us. But it is seldom denied that the New Testament mandates love for all. Love, in this case, is neither coterminous with nor dependent on hope. Of course the English preposition 'for' conceals a distinction which classical and other languages will make in their own terms: love 'for' is roughly love 'towards' whereas hope 'for' has a less secure English periphrasis, but certainly 'towards' is not apt. This, however, does not affect the present point. The point is the distinction between love and hope in relation to particulars.

---

[8] Leon Morris, *Testament of Love* (Grand Rapids, MI: Eerdmans, 1981), 258.

Turning to *agapē*, rather than to hope, it may seem tedious to rehearse familiar arguments for grounding social action in love. Yet I believe that a distinctive, if not original, presentation is in order. My strategy is to look at the prima facie case and tackle five objections to it. Space prevents me from essaying more than a minimal response to the objections, but the aim is adequate cogency not maximal rigour. The love which most naturally comes to mind in connection with the New Testament as far as social action is concerned is, of course, love for neighbour. Outside the three Synoptic accounts, it is found twice in Paul's epistles (Rom. 13:9; Gal. 5:14) and in James 2:8. Nothing in the following argument depends on claiming that the scope of 'neighbour' is intentionally or implicitly the same in all these cases. Nor is there any relevant point at issue if we take the canonical text without critical reconstruction as the basis of the following remarks. This consideration is of immediate relevance because the canonical *locus classicus* for the exposition of the commandment to love neighbour is the parable we know as the parable of the Good Samaritan. At first the neighbour in the parable is apparently identified by and even defined in terms of need. But, of course, in the account Jesus eventually identified the self, not the other, with 'neighbour'. This has its own potential in relation to social action if the aim is to weave together canonical strands. The implication of identifying the self, or active self, with the 'neighbour' seems to be this: the self is not essentially an individual contingently related to the other, but essentially person-in-relationship. That itself states a powerful principle of indiscrimination in relation to others, the relation from my side being determined by my identity as neighbour. This invites reflection on the nature of God of whom neither *elpis* nor *pistis* can usefully be predicated on the basis of New Testament linguistic or conceptual usage, but who is *agapē* according to John. And if we have gone so far as to fuse Johannine with Lucan concerns and Pauline concepts we could then connect the fundamentally relational character of the self with the fundamentally relational character of a deity who is love precisely in His inner-divine relationship, according to a trinitarian reading of the canon.

But whatever the possibilities of such a broad scheme, a less theologically indulgent reading of Luke will suffice to make the present point. To be a neighbour or to love another is to meet the need of the needy according to the need when the needy is met. A familiar way of stating social implications runs like this. Improving travel safety and communications, securing protection and legal sanction against felons, providing adequate health care, all seem to be not only legitimate but even mandatory extensions if possible of the Good Samaritan's programme. If it is the oppressive structure that causes another's misery then love for neighbour is exercised in the deliberate attempt to change structures. It is this kind of scenario we have in mind when using terms like 'social concern', 'social action' or 'social responsibility'.

Now this move from the parable to the conclusion drawn can be described in more than one way. Firstly, it might be argued that it is a matter of intuitive or imaginative application: the parable is the paradigm for situations which we recognize when they arise and the appropriate form of activity is readily grasped. That fits in with the way in which, for example, Dodd and Jeremias stressed the significance of parable as opposed to systematic exposition, but it is also consistent with the view taken in Chilton and McDonald's recent work whose concerns are especially germane to the theme of this essay.[9] But secondly, it might be urged that if the move from parable to application be warranted, clear inference is required. It may be held that features of the New Testament materials block such an inference so that to speak of the above type of social action as biblically warranted is wrong. So we examine five counter-arguments.

1. The New Testament never mandates a neighbour-love which entails attempts to transform structures. However you describe the relation of Old to New Testaments, its silence prohibits the kind of move earlier made.

Reference to the Old Testament is important here because by 'biblical' perspective I effectively mean 'New Testament' in this essay. That, however, will not distort the argument. As it stands, the above objection is insufficient. For what is proposed is that the biblical principle of neighbour-love permits and even mandates social action under amenable circumstances. The issue turns on the scope of the principle not the specificity of biblical materials. As an independent objection, then, this does not stand.

2. The New Testament on the whole proposes an attitude to established authority that is one of submission, which, when we consider

---

[9] B. Chilton and J. I. H. McDonald, *Jesus and the Ethics of the Kingdom* (London: SPCK, 1987).

its ramifications, discourages attempted transformation of the social order.

This point, indeed, can be alternatively formulated but the response to it should cover the alternatives. This objection, at best, cannot of itself do more than address the question of limits and methods of social action. In both Old and New Testaments, established authority is itself, within or without the covenant community, responsible for elements of social justice. There are divine criteria for responsible exercise of authority which entail the self-reformation of government when these are not met. The question, then, is not whether social structures may or should be transformed; it is about the relation of subject to authority in relation to such transformation. In passing, it is worth noting that even where one seems to get least encouragement for socially reforming activity, for example, 1 Peter, it is arguable that there is more to it than meets the twentieth-century eye.[10] But it suffices to note for the moment that, again, the objection is insufficient though of course it does indicate the issue at the cutting edge of much socio-political activity.

3. The primary responsibility of the Christian church is evangelism, not social action.

Again, significant reformulations and variations on this point are forthcoming. And again, an issue which is raised here, viz., the question of priorities and relations between evangelism and social action, cannot be addressed. The general difficulty with this objection or similar ones is that it does not reflect adequately on the point of evangelism. The epistle to the Romans is framed by the phrase 'obedience of faith' (1:4; 16:26) and it would suit my argument here to take this as a subjective genitive but the evidence is just not compelling enough. So instead let us just note what the Great Commission (Matthean) implies about the obedience of discipleship. Here discipleship is an aim of evangelism. One must then ask what lies at the heart of discipleship? We are presumably meant to glean this from Matthew's own Gospel. And love of neighbour is a strong candidate in this connection, allied, of course, to the love of God. If discipleship is a goal of evangelism and neighbour-love is crucial in discipleship and social action is taken to be a form of neighbour-love then evangelism and social action cannot be rivals at heart. Those who

---

[10] See Bruce Winter, 'The Public Honouring of Christian Benefactors', *JSNT* 34 (1988): 87–103; and 'Seek the Welfare of the City: Social Ethics according to 1 Peter', *Themelios* 13.3 (1988).

restrict the purpose of evangelism to getting others to heaven or to making others fishers of men need to integrate the robust requirement that we love our neighbour into that scheme without restricting the scope of love. This involves for one thing accepting that discipleship here on earth is attentive to material elements of life. It involves for another distancing the church from that prestigious Academy which elects Fellows whose sole aim is the election of other Fellows (though conscientious indulgence in statutory fraternal convivialities is also a preferred norm of conduct). So again, while the objection raises an issue which must be faced in a more comprehensive context, it is insufficient as it stands.

4. The social dimension of *agapē* in the early Christian communities was expressed in the form of love for brethren; the church, not the world, is the focus of the conscious social application of *agapē*.

We need not rehearse here the appeal that can readily be made to Johannine and Pauline literature. At root the question is: is any limitation of *agapē* in that literature a principled limitation in relation to society or is it a circumstantial limitation? The attempt to formulate a single principle to meet this objection adequately within our limits of space is formidable. Serious pursuit of this objection requires an appraisal of Käsemann's work (he reads Johannine literature as evidence of a relatively ingrown love) and recently the work of those like Beker and Rowland who observe a tension between some Pauline principles, pregnant with social radicalism, and Pauline social conservatism, disappointingly expressed in some other theological statements of principle.[11] Yet reflection on the concept of *agapē* in both John and Paul tends to turn aside the objection.

The point is this: clearly in John and implicitly, I think, in Paul, love is a principle of conduct only because it is a principle of identity.[12] This might be put another way but its substance is as follows. In Johannine literature the love which is meant to take root in the Christian life is not just a response to God and not just the human fruit of union with the Father through the Son. It is participation in the divine *agapē* so that the perichoretic relations of Father and Son described in John 17

---

[11] See J. C. Beker, *Paul the Apostle* (London: T&T Clark, 1980); this way of putting it draws rather on C. Rowland, *Christian Origins* (London: SPCK, 1985), 4.4.

[12] Cf. P. Tillich, *Systematic Theology* (Chicago: University of Chicago Press, 1963), 3:290.

are extended to believers. Of course this needs careful description. But on any interpretation—and one thinks not only of John 17 but of the extraordinary language of 1 John 4:12—love is a rule of conduct only as it constitutes anew the very spiritual life of believers, the identity of those reborn from above. A parallel point is harder to establish in the case of Paul partly because of the relative placing of *pistis* and *agapē*. Yet in the Galatian correspondence, the life of faith is most profoundly described as the life of the indwelling Christ (2:17–20) and the operation of faith, and hence of the indwelling Christ through the Spirit, is expressly pre-eminently love (5:6). Still, it is with reference to the letter to the Ephesians, whatever we may decide on authorship, that our point is best secured. It describes in unrivalled terms the eschatological foundation of doxology, the eschatology here normally being dubbed 'realized'. The believer's *agapē* to which the epistle refers is the sheer overflow of communion with Jesus Christ. Now a phenomenological reflection that does justice to this testimony would have to conclude that *agapē* in principle cannot possibly be restricted, because it marks one's identity. Love cannot be restricted to the church more than what one is one can be only in relation to the church and not to the world. It is certainly in order to argue, as many do, that the proper exegesis of Pauline and Johannine texts shows that love is not restrictive in the way some propose. But without prejudice to the results of such exegesis, it must be granted that any universalism of love is propounded in a context where intra-communal love is to the fore. The point is adequately secured if it is granted that principles of conduct and principles of identity are related in the proposed way. It follows that if social action is described as a way of applying *agapē* to those outside the church, then it is circumstance and not principle that accounts for such restriction as we find in John and Paul. At least, in the case of Paul, this obtains if we accept that the love described in Ephesians really does express a latency in the *agapē* of which he writes elsewhere.[13]

---

[13] Love includes care for bodily welfare as both Paul and John (at least in 1 John) make clear. With reference to circumstantial restrictions on love, the 'circumstances' in mind are those of first century Christianity in its social and political context as a community of love. Of course, I have not sought to indicate the positive aspect of the community ethic of early Christianity where it might be emphasized that the logical first place for the social expression of love is on principle, and not just circumstantially, the Christian community.

5. The final objection is listed as final for two closely related reasons. First, it touches on something behind all the objections we have surveyed so far, namely that of the background *Weltanschauung* in the New Testament documents for the life and work of love. Secondly, it explicitly leads us back to the relation of eschatology to love. The objection is this: if we interpret love of neighbour in the proposed way, relating it to social action, it collides with a vital strand of New Testament eschatology. It collides with premillenial belief. Such an eschatology, it may be urged, is pessimistic about the world, regarding it as bound to evil and deterioration from which there is salvation only in the Church faithful to Jesus until in his advent he destroys the evil and establishes the good. Hence, the argument goes, any intentionally structure-transforming love is misguided, confusing temporal endeavour with eschatological guarantee.

Of course, premillenial eschatology is not to be regarded as a monolith and even common doctrinal tenets may permit different consequences according to the different tenants of that position. One rebuttal is obviously denial of the premise, that is denial that premillenialism is a proper interpretation of any strand of New Testament material. But supposing the premillennialist interpretation were accepted, it could still be argued that the prospect of world-decline is not entailed in adoption of the premillenialist view of Christ's advent. And again, supposing it were granted that there is evidence in the New Testament of belief in such decline, it would not follow from this that nothing should be attempted and that nothing could succeed socially. Here we must invoke the earlier discussion of particulars. Just as surely as the future cosmic whole is not the sum of particulars, so there is no exegetical basis for interpreting any 'world-declining' strands in the New Testament in terms of all particulars. Even with wars and rumours of wars it does not follow that no wars will cease this side of the eschaton or that peacemaking is futile. Sure enough, as God may promise the success of temporally particular endeavours so he may foretell the doom of temporally particular endeavours. But it remains the case that even were the 'world-declining' position accepted, it would not rob love of its responsibility or ability to secure something rather than nothing. One should not despair of all particulars and so cannot on any eschatological position refuse love's labours.[14]

My response to the premillenial objection may appear to compound two difficulties at least in the thesis advanced so far. Firstly, it looks as if foundations for social responsibility are being laid with an express intention of avoiding eschatology. Love is being detached from eschatology by the ploy of saying that it is consistent with many interpretations. And that is an exercise in dogmatic rather than in biblical theology. Secondly, it looks as if we purchase the mandate for social action at the price of an extremely vague and even shifting idea of what social action embraces: it seems to be a general application of the parable of the Good Samaritan with a nod in the direction of structural transformation. So what is at stake in contemporary discussion of social responsibility never comes to light. If these two points are taken in order it will bring into sharper focus the contours of the present thesis.

On the first point, it is undeniable that eschatological perspectives in the New Testament qualify its description of love, though the extent of this is debatable.[15] Ogletree's appeal that we take to heart the eschatological horizon of biblical moral understanding (embracing love) is compatible with everything said so far.[16] Nothing as ambitious as the aim to relate eschatology to ethics is being attempted here. That would raise a host of questions on ethics in relation to expectation of the Parousia; the ethics of rewards and punishments; ethics and realized eschatology, etc. The declared interest in the relation of social activity to the future cosmic, overall perspective is just the first of many limitations in the argument. Certainly such a perspective is needed to describe love properly. All love's operations are framed by what God will accomplish, fulfil and realize in or for human history. Love can be sustained, enriched and informed by hope. To it may be promised the revelation of the intelligibility of its work in the eschaton. The relation of

---

[14] Whilst it does not affect our treatment, it should be noted that no one denies the historically socially effective activity of premillenialists though it may be claimed that eschatology and action do not make happy logical bedfellows in such cases: C. Sugden and V. Samuel, eds., *The Church in Response to Human Need* (Oxford: Regnum Press, 1987), 152.

[15] See B. Gerhardsson, *The Ethos of the Bible* (London: Darton, Longman & Todd, 1980), esp. 33f.

[16] *The Use of the Bible in Christian Ethics* (Minneapolis, MN: Fortress Press, 1983).

love and hope can be illuminated by the introduction of other concepts, like *hupomonē*. These things and their importance is not denied. But the whole point of refusing to adjudicate issues of biblical eschatology is to establish the logic of love, viz., that it mandates social action even if hope is limited. Keeping eschatology open is a way of securing this principle.

The second point touches on the important matter of definition and clarification. 'Social action', for example, is often used rather generally if not vaguely in relevant literature, just as a multitude of conditions are covered by such a phrase as 'the poor and the oppressed'. Let us return to the Good Samaritan. The familiar suggestion was adopted that the logic of his concern for the individual entails an attack on social structures where they, rather than physical robbery, create hardship.[17] But equally the parable shows that any concern for structures is at heart concern for the individual whom they oppress, however many there are and however they are joined in community or society. This is a point too easily forgotten both when the concept of 'society' gets the spotlight and when suffering is treated arithmetically, as though there is a quantum of suffering that can be weighed in terms of number of sufferers.[18] The Good Samaritan, in reaching out for one, intentionally reaches out for all, for need and neighbourliness know no bounds. At the same time, in seeking structural transformation if it can help the needy, the Samaritan just implements the most effective way of meeting the individual in his or her need. 'Social action', then, principally refers to that activity which is directed to the alleviation of suffering and injustice where they find social expression, including action in relation to social structures. The point is not to map out spheres of action. The point is to identify generally but concretely the fact of human need and suffering and to argue that a relevant distinction between hope and love brings to light the grounds for responsibility and action.

If, now, a world-transforming project is really the quest to love the suffering individual, in line with the Good Samaritan parable, the

---

[17] It might be held that this is just the point: we ought to change people and not structures. But again, while we may debate the relation of evil in people to evil embedded in structures, there is no need to deny our responsibility for directly addressing the latter.

[18] That is, suffering cannot be quantified as if ten people injured amounts to ten times the suffering of one person injured. Ten times more for whom?

reason why particular eschatologies should not be overly obtrusive comes to light. If world-transforming desire is not a belief that society will improve but just a desire, for example, to feed those without bread, it is hard to see how the detail of eschatology should be allowed to thwart or enhance activity too much at this level. The same may be said in relation to the quest for justice in law. That boils down to the quest for just remand conditions, just processes of trial etc. To speak of such things as these being eschatologically transformed or perfected is, of course, unfortunate and inappropriate, if a moment's caricature be permitted! But to speak, on the other hand, as though a pessimistic *Weltanschauung* does away with any desire to achieve such things, or any attempts to do so, is worse than inappropriate. For these are precisely the kinds of particulars that need attention within any *Weltanschauung*. And surely these are precisely the kinds of particulars mandated by a biblical principle, that of neighbour-love. It is the very particularity in the biblical injunction to love coupled with reflection on the effective activity of love that impels us to assign to love a kind of independence of eschatology. Three qualifications may be introduced here. First, it is true that social action on behalf of the hungry or unjustly treated may be urged on grounds other than those mentioned, and that action in different social areas may be grounded in varied theological arguments. Secondly, it is true that there are areas where one's precise eschatological position tends to impinge on social action more than it does in others. An example is political liberation, where arguments on the concept of national self-determination go on. Thirdly, I do not deny that different ways of interpreting and applying biblical eschatology affects our social attitudes. My proposal is that we minimize the impact of particular eschatologies, particularly premillenial ones, by arguing for world-transforming *agapē* within its very framework.

A further point, however, should be pressed. 'Social action' is often taken to include action on behalf of non-human creation in its own right. That involves animals and environment. What has been said so far seems to cut this out, because we have talked about neighbours. Animals constitute an interesting and important case in this connection but they cannot be regarded as 'neighbour' from the biblical point of view, at least as the idea of 'neighbour' is taken up in the New Testament use of Leviticus.[19] While it is not my brief to expound comprehensively

---

[19] Though see the comments of C. Westermann on our humanity and dominion over animals, *Genesis 1–11* (London: SPCK, 1984), 159. But of course he does not call the animals neighbours.

the biblical bases for social responsibility, nor to do so in relation to the non-human world, it is worth remarking that if we respect the location of the precept 'love your neighbour' in the Synoptic tradition, we arrive at a ground of responsibility for non-human creation. For one sure sign of the limitation of our project is the detachment of talk about love of neighbour from talk of love of God. Love of God certainly entails care for what God cares for and that takes in the question of the non-human. Indeed, I should wish to argue that what has been said about love and hope, as regards the commitment of the one and the limitation of the other, applies, *mutatis mutandis*, to the non-human creation.

However, it is another feature of the injunction to love God that will detain us here as we come to a conclusion. Reflection on it suggests a further reason for placing love in relation to eschatology in the way proposed, though here an outline rather than demonstration must suffice. With talk of love of God we are brought back, as in the case of neighbour-love, to the Old Testament. All New Testament references to the two injunctions are presented in relation to law or commandment.[20] In Romans and Galatians, the dispensational sense of God's activity in the world is more marked than anywhere else in Pauline literature. Hence the effect of his introduction of neighbour-love in the latter part of both letters is to tempt us to suppose that love stands in relation to eschatology as the stable does to the shifting. Given an argument such as Zimmerli's, that the 'hope' of deuteronomic history is 'perhaps' and not promise, and given the plethora of strands in Old and New Testament eschatologies,[21] the temptation is rather strong. But one must hold back. For one thing, the bold will detect in the initial promise to Abraham after the disaster of Babel the plan for the course of all biblical eschatology in nuclear form.[22] For another, it can be said that the New Testament universalizes an intentionally restrictive concept of 'neighbour' in the Old Testament. So we resist the attempt to plot a stable love command in relation to a shifting eschatology.

But of course Paul does not speak in this connection of love for God. That command certainly does look stable. No increase or diminution in its scope seems possible. New Testament christology does not suggest it. It is precisely because of its majestic immutability that it is so impressive

---

[20] I use both words because actually Mark uses *entolē* but not *nomos*, loc. cit.

[21] See D. A. Hubbard, 'Hope in the Old Testament', *Tyndale Bulletin* 34 (1983): 40.

[22] Just in its implicit principle; see, e.g., W. Dumbrell, *The End of the Beginning* (New York: Lancer Books, 1985), 130f.

to find the command to love neighbour linked with it in the New Testament, however the connection be described.[23] In his classic *Agape and Eros,* Anders Nygren speaks of the 'spontaneous' and 'unmotivated' character of divine love towards us, spring of our grateful imitation in relation to our neighbour. It is not surprising that Nygren, like others, dwelt on the words of Matthew 5:45: 'He causes his sun to rise on the evil and the good, and sends rain on the righteous and the unrighteous.' The context is the command to love our enemies. Divine provision for life in this world is thus not contingent on the eschatological destiny of those for whom God provides. Love for this God arises in response to his infinite love manifested, it is true, in the election of a people, but manifested too in an activity that is loving, whether temporal projects rise or fall, irrespective of the eschatological destiny of the individual.[24]

Reflection on that love alerts us to a peril in the quest for motives of action other than those of love for God and neighbour. The way that quest is conducted often threatens to take the heart out of social action. Refraining from action is far more a crisis in the heart of love than a failure to get eschatology right in the head. The insistence of Beker, for example, that only if social activity can anticipate eschatological transformation is it really meaningful, is surely torpedoed by the rebellious rebuttal that to do unto others what we should have them do unto us is the law and the prophets.[25]

Love of God is rich in passion, desire for the glory of God and desire to do the will of God. What God desires for the world and will accomplish for it is set forth in the description of the eschaton. By its vision it kindles in those who love God the unquenchable desire that, as far as may be, God's will be done now on earth as it will be in the new earth and heaven. Christian hope, von Balthasar wrote, 'vibrates with the thought that the earth should reply to heaven in the way that heaven

---

[23] It is not suggested that Jesus first forged the link; indeed, it is explicitly the lawyer who does so in the Lucan account.

[24] This may be said in a way sufficiently general for our purposes without commitment to a particular interpretation of election or atonement.

[25] The whole argument of Beker on this point in *Paul's Apocalyptic Gospel* (Minneapolis, MN: Fortress Press, 1982) misfires if the argument of this lecture is valid.

has addressed the earth'.[26] Calculation and appraisal in terms of the eschaton may have their role in relation to social action but it is totally unsafe to let it play their role until the principles of love for God and neighbour have taken proper root in the heart. Given desire and given promise, love does indeed generate hope—the kind of hope that governs all particulars, though there is no promise and it is not that kind of hope which is conformed to promise. But it is not just wishful thinking either, though it is wish. It is hope embedded in the heart of a love allowed to form sheerly as love of God and neighbour; and only when love is given that independence will its own distinctive hopes be fruit that is good to eat. And among its fruits, rooted in the soil of biblical theology, is social activity . . . and if that is rooted in the will of God, it will accomplish whatever God purposes for it. If we believe that, we have ground for unremitting obedience in social responsibility.[27]

---

[26] Hans Urs von Balthasar, *Truth is Symphonic* (Ft. Collins, CO: Ignatius Press, 1987), 191.

[27] Liberation theologians may object that the whole argument of this lecture assumes that action follows reflection. The hermeneutical issues here are deep. It seems to me that the argument of the essay can accommodate this objection with minimal adjustment. This is achieved by saying that the whole of the foregoing simply captures a moment: the moment in the dialectical process of action-reflection when the latter is permitted to impinge on the former. If the proposed adjustment is hopelessly naïve then let the piece stand within the framework of the European bourgeois approach!

I am grateful to Dr. Will Strange for pointing out, in relation to the argument of this essay, that the notion of the Kingdom is conspicuous by its absence. The reason is that my aim is not to eliminate talk of hope or of the Kingdom in relation to social action, but both to establish limits to hope and to establish that such limits do not limit social action.

www.ingramcontent.com/pod-product-compliance
Ingram Content Group UK Ltd.
Pitfield, Milton Keynes, MK11 3LW, UK
UKHW041427180426
11947UKWH00007B/319